Kingdom Called

Joel Holm

ISBN: 0986181927
ISBN-13: 978-0986181924

DEDICATION

To David, for launching me into this journey years ago. To my favorite brothers, Simon, Josh and Daniel, for allowing me to come alongside. To Bayless, for trusting and inspiring me. To John, for standing with me. To Mark, Michael, Solomon, Ron, Nathan, Peter and so many others who have taught me, through their friendship and their faith, what it truly means to be Kingdom Called.

CONTENTS

ACKNOWLEDGMENTS

Thanks to Wendy for taking my ideas and making sense of them with words. To Giann, for his relentless creativity. To Marie, for her cruel yet highly valued red pen, separating fluff from truth. To the countless business leaders who teach me by example. To the many thinkers and authors upon whom some of my ideas are formed. And to you the reader, thanks for taking time to read this book. May it inspire you and challenge you to a greater calling for Christ and His Kingdom.

Introduction

Kingdom Called: Harnessing the Power of Business to Change the World. Why such a basic title? Google these words and you will discover a large amount of material on the topic of God's Kingdom and business. So why not come up with a more unique title? I tried but honestly what is needed is not fancier wrapping on the same issues but rather, a deeper understanding of God's design of business in the grand scheme of His Kingdom.

The purpose of this small book is to address the idea of Kingdom Business as it relates to both corporate institutions and the individual follower of Christ in the marketplace. I entitled it Kingdom Called because just as every church and pastor has a calling, so too every business and business leader has a Kingdom calling. Recent teachings have rightly focused on the role of the marketplace leader or the "Christian missionary in the workplace." But not enough has been said about the business institution being a creation of God for His Kingdom purpose, much like the church is a creation of God. What if business was as much a part of God's plan as His church? What if business has a critically important role to play in and of itself and not just as a means to a different end?

This book does not stand in contrast to most of the ideas that have surfaced in the recent years. I am grateful for all that has been developed over the years regarding business and God's Kingdom. And while Christians are growing in their understanding and value for business's role in God's mission, there is still more to His idea of Kingdom Business that we have yet to discover.

Having spent the better part of the past five years working with entrepreneurs and business leaders (who are also followers of Christ) I've discovered five critical issues always come up, regardless of the individual, the industry or the cultural, regional context.

3

These five issues are:

1. God's Idea of Kingdom Business

2. The Biblical Distinction of Kingdom Business

3. How to Build a Kingdom Business

4. Family and Kingdom Business

5. Kingdom Business and the Local Church

In chapter one, I address the biblical idea of Kingdom Business. Work seems to get lost as a significant story line in the Creation story. The Bible teaches on the role of the economy (business, money, wealth, ownership, competition, profit, etc.) for God's Kingdom purpose. These issues are not just issues of personal choice but need to be seen in light of God's greater agenda for His Kingdom.

In chapter two, I address the core principles that form the identity of Kingdom Business. These five truths distinguish Kingdom Business from other business. Kingdom Business is not identified by wealth creation or wealth distribution (although both are important). Rather Kingdom Business is rooted in spiritual distinctions that are clearly laid out in Scripture as Paul wrote to the economic workforce of the early church.

In chapter three, I get down to the practical outworking of Kingdom Business as much as is possible in such a short book. You already have a business strategy. That doesn't change. But the execution of Kingdom Business requires an integrated approach that enhances your business' identity, involves the people connected to the business and takes on community initiatives as part of your business' work. Building a Kingdom Business is about recognizing what God is already doing through your profit-making business, and stewarding that for even more benefit to the community.

In chapter four, I address the more personal aspect of Kingdom Business, the role of the family. Spiritually and practically you should not separate your family from your work. As a business owner, this topic involves determining inheritance, the role of generations and transitioning the family business and how a family can do ministry together. Even if you are not a Kingdom Business owner, you should find much of the chapter applicable to your own family.

In chapter five, I address the relationship between the Kingdom Business leader and the local church. This relationship is the proverbial "800 pound gorilla" in the room that business leaders and pastors are hesitant to address. This chapter discusses the problem, the various roles needed for God's joint purpose, and the most effective way for a business and church to go beyond "co-existing" to become genuine partners for God's Kingdom.

At the end of each chapter, I've included a few questions for discussion and further study or application. The best way marketplace leaders will grow in their understanding of God's purpose is to interact with other marketplace leaders while leading a Kingdom Business. Hopefully, the ideas in these chapters and the questions and application that follow will help guide you in this pursuit.

Chapter One

God's Story For Your Life

"Without vision my people perish."

I love a good story. I was watching a movie awhile back on an airplane called *A Beautiful Mind,* starring Russell Crowe. It's an intriguing story, but half way through the movie, the audio/visual equipment of the plane shut down. And for the remainder of the flight it never rebooted, so there I was left hanging in the middle of the story, with no resolve, no sense of purpose or completion because I couldn't watch the end of the story! I thought to myself, "What would *life* be like if you missed out on half of God's story for your life and you were left hanging, wondering what the full storyline is?"

Many business owners and leaders understand this sense. Your spiritual story is told in part – the very important part of you being a sinner and needing Christ – but not in full as you rarely are told God's story for your life as a business leader. That part is also very important.

Proverbs says that without vision people perish. That statement doesn't mean that we will die without vision, rather it means we lose heart. Our shoulders shrug; we have a hard time getting motivated for anything. Not having a vision is not having a conviction or any energy for life. In some ways it's a picture of our relationship with work when we only know half our story. Without a vision for our work we perish. But if we can capture a vision – wow! Then we become an unstoppable force. Having a clear vision does something. It creates in a way that helps us ignore obstacles, as we keep focused on that end result we have so clearly in our sights. We will make sacrifices that may not even feel like sacrifices because we have a vision in our minds and our hearts that is crystal clear.

In this book, I want to show you the vision God has for your business and how your business, your work, and commerce play an important role in God's story for this world. I want to help you capture a little bit of God's vision for your life.

Scene One: It's All Good

Since I love a good movie and a good story, I figured that I would pattern our understanding of God's creation of business and your Kingdom Calling as a story. All stories have an arc and follow the same general pattern. The story begins with a first scene where life is good. Everything is being established and all is well. People are happy. There are no problems. There is no conflict. That's how our life story starts. Genesis 1:1 says, "In the beginning God created the heavens and the earth." Please note, our first glimpse of God is of Him at work. But God never works alone. So Genesis 1:26 says, "So then God said, "Let Us make mankind in Our image and in Our likeness so that they may rule over the earth." It's really important to understand that in your story, you were made in the image of God for the purpose of work; you were made to be like Him. That's why He created you and crafted you the way He did. That's why He gave you the gifts and personality that He gave you. And God did all this before sin and destruction ever entered the story.

Genesis 1:28 says, "God blessed them: 'Prosper! Reproduce! Fill earth! Take charge! Be responsible for my creation." Then Genesis 2 tells the story again but from a different perspective. God does a corporate strategic analysis of what He's done. He assesses His work. He says, "It is good, it is not good, it is very good," paraphrasing of course. It's as if God is evaluating Himself. He looks at His work coming to the conclusion and sees that His creation is good but it's not quite good enough, something more is needed. Genesis 2:5 explains that there was no one to work the ground. Ah, problem identified. Not quite good enough yet.

But why does the ground need to be worked? Isn't that part of the fall? Didn't the ground get cursed and thus have to be worked? The sequence of a story is important. The ground was cursed and work changed, but be clear that work began as part of God's perfect design for His creation.

God sees that there's no one to work this ground so God places Adam in the garden and creates a special coworker, Eve. Genesis 2:7-8 states, "Then the Lord God formed a man from the dust of the ground and breathed into his nostrils the breath of life, and the man became a living being. Now the Lord God had planted a garden in the east, in Eden; and there He put the man He had formed." See, here it is! We were created to do work before sin ever reared its ugly face on this earth. Why? We were designed for work because of God's vision for us being made in His Image. He works so we work.

I (and others) call it the Creation Mandate. God created and engineered us to co-create and reflect who He is. Furthermore, it's critical to understand that God's plan for us, His Creation Mandate, was never retracted because of sin. It was never retracted with Christ. It was never retracted with the Great Commission. It's still in play today and the Bible teaches that it's still in play throughout our entire story.

When God says to "subdue the earth," what He's actually saying is to rule over this beautiful creation in likeness of Him through work, for the benefit of human kind. To subdue literally means "gain profit" from the earth. Have you ever carefully read God's description of the Garden of Eden? Do you know what it describes? It describes trees and waters and minerals. It describes Eden full of raw materials. It's like God says, "Here is all the raw materials, now go to work. Cultivate these raw materials to fulfill all the potential of this earth so all humanity can flourish for the benefit of all."

I consulted with a family owned business involved in real estate development. They buy property, build large condominium buildings and then sell the units in the retail housing market. They start with raw materials (building supplies) and if they manage it well (stewardship of resources, including labor) they will make a strong profit, while providing safe homes for families. This is what

God is telling us to do in the beginning of our story. Life is good. But we weren't created with a finished product. The Garden is not completed. We have this idea that the Garden of Eden was like a city park. It was all manicured and laid out perfectly, and all God needed was for someone to pick up a piece of garbage here and there. Adam and Eve are seen as tending an existing garden not creating a civilization. But God describes His Garden as a rich forest, full of all raw materials with Adam and Eve put in there to work it for the purpose of creation and stewardship in harmony with God, in the likeness of God.

It's as if God says, "Take all these raw materials and make something amazing for humankind." The Garden was designed for the benefit of humankind and the first glimpse of our work is this activity of reigning and ruling so that humankind can profit from the raw materials God has provided through creation.

Humans were created to uniquely reflect God through work, which is interesting because there was still no evil or sin at this point in the story. Why would we need to reflect God? We always think of reflecting God's image because there are people who don't know Him and who need to see Him. But there were no sinners yet. Nonetheless, we were created to reflect Him.

We were created by God to exercise authority over creation. Why do we need this authority? Why did God create us? Listen to me friends. Scene one of our lives is really good because God's work and relationship with us is not defined by sin. God, as part of our created identity, designed work for us to co-create and reflect Him. God created us for His purpose.

As much as you may sometimes feel like it was, work was not part of the fall. Creation was not a ridiculously early retirement plan that got ruined with sin. Work was before sin, during sin, and after sin was eradicated. Work is forever, as work is part of our eternal living as well. Why is it that we minimize work, when God doesn't?

Being so much a part of His creation, you conclude that your work and your business are not just human choice. Your work and your business are not just necessary evils to live. They are divine in initiative and in purpose. That's why when you work you are Kingdom Called. Work is how you were hard-wired by God. Work is a key component to His formula for your fulfillment and for furthering His Kingdom.

Grab a Bible real quick and take a look at Leviticus 26. God describes His view of abundance and success for us. He calls it "living in the blessing." Folks, the first thing He describes is bringing the rains at the right time. Why? So they could work the land and live in the land of plenty. Even blessing and abundance are defined by the opportunity to work. Notice the other promises He offers when we operate in His plan. Huge blessings come from God through work. That's why He created us to work. That's how our story began. However, we know that every good story has an antagonist and ensuing conflict.

Scene Two: It's All Bad

Scene two. Enter Satan and enter sin. Sin taints everything good that God created into something bad. This is true of emotions, sex, profit, and yes, work. Sin against God's created design has serious consequences on the work that He created for us for to do. Genesis 3:17-19 states: "Cursed is the ground because of you; through painful toil you will eat food from it all the days of your life. It will produce thorns and thistles for you, and you will eat the plants of the field. By the sweat of your brow you will eat your food until you return to the ground, since from it you were taken; for dust you are and to dust you will return." Have you ever been frustrated by work, the toil of it, the frustration, the physical and emotional pain? All of that is the consequence of sin.

A recent American television show that illustrates this is Dirty Jobs with Mike Rowe. The television host finds people who do the most disgusting, filthy jobs and he joins them in their work. That's a picture of sin with a bit of comedy woven through it. Who would ever want to do this kind of work? People hate their jobs and even if you don't hate your job, every one of us have some incredibly difficult moments in our work.

Because of sin, work became very difficult in ways that were not part of its original design. But this is also true of marriage, health, parenting, and so much more in life. The Bible says very clearly in Genesis 3 that because of sin, in work there would now be incredible hardships. You'll get paid but work, like all of life, faces the consequence of sin that ravaged this world.

Think of it. Think of your business and the difficulty of much of it. Think about how litigation affects your operations. Consider all the wasted hours and resources that go into insurance protection, often to protect you from an outworking of sin. Think of bureaucracy that has to be put into place because we don't trust each other. All commitments must be framed in triplicate with legal entanglements because people's vows are not trustworthy. Think of corruption in many parts of the world and how it dictates who can benefit, leaving so many who cannot benefit from work. Think even of the weather and how it affects work. Consider the people you work with and how hard it is at times to work with them, often, by their sin-driven behavior.

All of these consequences of sin have influenced us to believe that we work only so that we can eat, pay our bills and live. We have determined that work is a misery we must endure until we get to Heaven, or at least have enough money to retire on. Work can't possibly be godly as it is so full of sin in so many ways. So Christians, join in a unified chorus with people of all faiths, and together in one voice we pronounce, "Thank God it's Friday!" This is a statement that knows now religious boundaries. Those who do not have vision will perish. Their shoulders will shrug and they'll barely get up on a Monday morning to endure for another week.

In this scene the enemy is celebrating. You want to know why? It's because he has shut down the Creation Mandate. Co-create and reflect no longer exist for us. There is only drudgery and toil. And with that, we lose that abundant life that God planned for us. It's like a fallow piece of prime real estate. So much benefit and beauty can come of it, but for now it sits as nothing but a weed filled spot of land benefiting no one and acting only as an eye sore.

Have you ever seen a vacant lot? At one point workers were digging a deep hole. Maybe they even had the foundation poured. Then the money ran out. The workers left. Weeds grew. Iron rusted. The lot sits, not only vacant but a horrible eyesore in the community. It serves no productive function. Worse than that, it becomes a detriment to the community. It lowers property values. It can even be dangerous. But what if someone with vision bought that property? What if someone stepped in to refinance it and brought jobs to the community. What if through its renewed construction, the life of the community was enhanced? What gratitude that community would have for whoever would come in and restore that piece of property.

That's a picture of our next scene. Work needs to be redeemed. It needs a hero and whenever you watch a movie, you know that scene where the hero will swoop in and save the day. You wait on the edge of your seat, knowing the hero is coming yet the tension builds until you can hardly take it anymore. You even have an expectation of what that hero is going to look like. You know the size of his muscles. You can predict how this hero will save the village.

Scene Three: Enter the Hero

Scene three is when our hero finally shows up to save us from the horrors of drudgery and toil, but he doesn't look anything like we thought he would. Do you know what Jesus comes as when He shows up on the scene? He comes as a businessman, a carpenter. Have you ever wondered why God sent this spiritually perfect hero as...a carpenter? He is after all the Master Craftsman of the universe. But did you wonder why God's plan was that Jesus would spend most of his life on earth crafting tables as a business? Even in Mark 6 the religious leaders question Jesus' religious worthiness because He was from the marketplace. "Isn't this the carpenter?" they question incredulously.

Why would Jesus spend the majority of his years working at a job? Ironically the church today tells carpenters if you want to be spiritual, go to church. Jesus magnificently flips it and tells carpenters "If you want to be spiritual, make really good tables for people." Think of Jesus today. He would be a clerk, accountant, a handyman, a banker, a teacher, a farmer, or a business owner. Jesus would do what you do. He would live in the apartment complex you live in. It would be a part of His identity. It would be a part of His calling as a hero. Even Superman had a day job.

First John 2:2 states, "He is the atoning sacrifice for our sins, and not only for ours but also for the sins of the whole world." He died for you individually but guess what? He also conquered sin and evil over the world. Our job was to rule over the earth in peaceful prosperity. We were to take this raw material and craft it into something that would benefit all of God's creation. But we didn't get the job done - despite many good opportunities. The world was broken. We became abusers of creation, not reigning co-laborers with God. We failed in the Creation Mandate. Yet God does something so beautiful as an act of grace with our divine employment. When our Hero comes, He doesn't fire us for our poor labor. Instead, He redeems us. He doesn't replace us with machines that will do a better job. He restores us back to the glorious destiny God intended for us even though we willfully blew every opportunity He had given us.

I had a friend who was the worst worker ever! For those of you who own your businesses, I would never suggest you to hire my friend. Actually I'd warn you of him. One company did hire him and not surprisingly he called me a month later to tell me that he had been fired. Duh! Then he asked me, "Would you call my manager and see if he'd take me back?" I quickly told my friend, "No I'm not going to do that; you deserved to be fired."

Like my friend, we deserved to be replaced when it came to the Creation Mandate, but God in His mercy didn't do that. He redeemed us and restored us so that the original Creation Mandate can continue to be fulfilled, by us. The Son of God came to do what Adam was supposed to do. The Son creates and reflects. Jesus recreates us and reflects His heavenly Father to us. He says if you see Me, you have seen the Father. If you hear Me, you have heard the Father. He restores us and then equips us like never before, by filling us with the Holy Spirit of God. Now we are set to once again co-create and reflect God. We are back to being Kingdom Called.

Jesus comes to redeem us and He also cares greatly about society. He taught his disciples to pray "give us this day our daily bread." There is a social aspect to this prayer. For everyone to have daily bread there must be a thriving economy, fair employment and social justice. To pray for daily bread is to pray against exploitation in trade, business, labor and government. To pray this prayer is to commit to answer this Lord's Prayer. It means to recognize the work of Jesus and accept your role in fulfilling His Creation Mandate.

Scene Four: Enter You

Back to our movie. If you've seen a lot of movies, you know the hero shows up and usually, single handedly saves the day. But at some point, the villagers realize who the true hero is and often at the last possible moment, the villagers join the hero in his crusade against evil. "Freedom," cries William Wallace from Braveheart and the men on horseback ride! Here's where you are now in real time in the unfolding movie of your life story.

You...we are the villagers. We join the hero. You know why this scene is so important? For those of you reading this book, there are easily hundreds of industries represented. Every one of these industries are broken. Each of them needs a hero, a hero sent from heaven. Christ redeemed our spirit but He also restored our purpose. You see, the Great Commission is about helping people find their way to Jesus so they can have a relationship with God. But the Great Commission did not remove or replace God's Creation Mandate.

The church and all its members are responsible for carrying out that Great Commission, reaping that great harvest, but Kingdom Business is responsible for carrying out the Creation Mandate right alongside it. So what does the Creation Mandate in scene four look like when we join God in His work? What does that mean? Let me help you capture the vision by showing you an example.

I have a friend who owns a business that provides business-to-business marketing. One of the business's clients is a cancer treatment center. When a person is diagnosed with cancer, one of the greatest hardships is knowing how to navigate the maze of doctors, insurance coverage and treatment scenarios. This labyrinth of confusion creates great fear and despair that plagues many patients. This cancer treatment center however centralizes all the treatment. They want to make the process easier and stress-free for their patients. However they needed a clear and inspiring script for their representatives to use in talking patients through the process.

When a patient calls the treatment center, one operator guides him or her through the process from start to finish. My friend's role, through his company, was to write the script for that process. In talking Creation Mandate with him, I pointed out how uniquely God had positioned him. Tens of thousands of people, facing a great struggle, lose hope when trying to process this overwhelming task. Now these patients will be guided in a process that will bring hope and peace and faith. And this script is crafted by my friends' business.

This is truly a Kingdom Calling. This is the Creation Mandate. Help society to flourish. Create and reflect God in doing so. My friend's business is also flourishing. Fulfilling God's purpose and being profitable are not diametrically opposed. In Kingdom Business they work together. Through his business, my friend is serving God's purpose and bringing God's blessing (faith, hope, peace of mind) to God's creation.

Even better, God is being blessed by this work. Almost any business endeavor, except the ones that destroy society like the adult entertainment industry, can be seen in view of the Creation Mandate and helping society to flourish. Some are easier to capture in our mind. Some are harder. That's where faith comes in. If you make signs, you are adding to the flourishing of a local economy. Your business signs matter. If you own a house cleaning business, you are providing cleanliness and service to families. In the Creation Mandate you must believe that your business matters to God and that it is a gift to God Himself. Let me explain.

Work done in line with the Creation Mandate (co-create and reflect) blesses the business owner/worker with profits of multiple kinds that we'll address in the next chapter, but it also blesses others. In this way, it becomes like a gift or form of worship to God. You see, when you catch the vision of the Creation Mandate to co-create (reign, prosper, flourish) and you reflect (show the world His character, love, help, and blessing) through business, this is a gift to God.

You are walking in His original purpose for you and joining Him in His grand design. This makes your work a form of worship to Him. Your business becomes mission.

Business *is* Mission

The idea of business and God's Kingdom is not a new one. Christians were slow in recognizing how God has used business throughout our history. There is still much progress to be made but we are on our way. However its important we don't stop learning how and why God created business, thinking we have arrived to a full understanding of Kingdom Business.

For example, most teaching on Kingdom business focuses on one of three ways God's work takes place in the marketplace. We have these ideas that business can be for God if it operates in these three ways. One way is Business *and* Mission. This is when business enables you to do mission. The often-used example is that of the Apostle Paul making tents that allowed him to do God's work. Then there is Business *as* Mission. This is where a business meets a specific, targeted need such as women with AIDS who make and sell jewelry to pay for their medications. And finally there is Business *for* Mission. This is where business is viewed solely for its profits that go to support mission work. Examples of this are the numerous micro-enterprise models that exist, especially in developing world regions. Let me be clear. I am so grateful for each of these definitions of the role of Kingdom Business. Each serves an important function in God's Kingdom.

But the vision I want you to catch is not represented by these three ideas. Kingdom Business means that business in itself can be mission! Business *is* mission.

Business is not just about the individual as a marketplace missionary, nor is business only a means to an end for God's mission. Rather, Business *is* Mission. This means the very identity of a business as an institution was created by God for His Kingdom. And by its very nature business serves its purpose in the Kingdom. Business can be both profitable and Kingdom ministry, at the same time, doing its one work. Actually, a business's profitability is one way of showing how effective that business is in its Kingdom ministry. Business is not just a means to an end. Business is bigger than just the worker. Business, as an institution, just as the local church as an institution, is designed by God to help build His Kingdom (co-create) and glorify God (reflect). A Kingdom Business is a gift, an act of worship to God.

Work is Worship

You may not realize this, but you were hardwired to worship. We all worship something or someone. I was watching a video clip with my kids, where thousands of young people had their hands stretched in the air, crying and singing out with ultimate abandon in pure, focused worship. I was thinking how we were watching some of the best worshipers in the world. The sad part was that they were worshipers at a teen idol rock concert, not at a church. Regardless, they were still some of the best worshipers I've ever seen. They just weren't worshiping God. We are wired for worship. It's part of our created identity.

So, if we are hardwired by God to worship Him and work with Him, it's a fair conclusion, that work is one of our primary ways we worship God. Our business is a Kingdom Business and a gift to

Him, not just because we give a percentage of the profits away. No. Kingdom Business is our worship to God because our business is following His created design. And, as is always the case with God, He loves to bless those who worship Him. With God's way, it's win-win-win-win. An opportunity to do His will in a major area of life must be taken seriously. His opportunities always lead to the path He has designed for us. When we serve Him with loyalty, humility and diligence, God will open doors for even greater blessing. Your business, in line with His principles and His design, can be an act of worship to God.

Your story can be a beautiful one, one that God sits with His popcorn in his plush recliner enjoying each unfolding moment. The story had its rough moments with a villain who wanted to permanently ruin a beautiful idea called "work". He found a way to twist a beautiful idea and make it corrupt and agonizing, so much so that the ideal dream is to never have to work again. How wrong that was. How ugly things got. But the hero came in and saved the day. Once our eyes were opened, we the villagers are now here to walk in His victory and live happily ever, working each day with vision and life.

Now we're not quite living His story fully in our lives yet, but as Christ followers we are called to live and see by faith. Actually, if you read the end of this story, in the Happily Ever After the work never stops. Work is designed as such a gift and blessing that God lets us keep it in heaven. My large screen TV won't qualify for eternity. In comparison to the high def visuals that will be there, my TV will be pathetic. But work - it stays. It will just be better than we could ever imagine. You work in heaven. The Great Commission stops but work doesn't. Work continues on from Genesis through Revelation and onwards because work is part of God's divine nature. We are wired and created by God to work.

Can you imagine what this world would look like if there were a few billion Creation Mandate stories? If each believer caught the vision that his or her work really matters to God and to His creation? What if each Christ follower could say with great conviction, "I was put on this earth by God, designed and filled by his Spirit, to fulfill His Creation Mandate, to create and rule over this earth so people can flourish in His love and God be glorified."

What if every Christian business owner would say, "My business is called by God as in an integral part of His Kingdom." Now that would be a vision. That would be an award-winning story!

Questions

1. Do you feel your business is operating at its maximum capacity in its Kingdom Calling?

2. How will it change your view when you go to work, to see your work as worship and your business as a Kingdom Business?

3. Can you redefine your business, reflecting God, and showing how your business is in line with His Creation Mandate?

Chapter Two

The Five Distinctions of Kingdom Business

"Unless the Lord builds the house,
the builders labor in vain."

What will it look like for you to work as worship? What would it take to transform your business so that business *is* mission? What is your Kingdom Business? Now that we've explored the concept that business is mission, it's critical to identify what a Kingdom Business is, as opposed to a traditional business. You can build the most profitable, successful business that the world has ever known, but if it's not a Kingdom Business, the Bible says it will be hollow. Worse, in more places than one, the Bible talks about the profits of the wicked being handed over to the righteous. I am not saying that you are wicked and somehow others more deserving will get your money. I am saying it's wise to learn from one of the wealthiest, wisest and most renowned business leaders in all of biblical history about your business. Let's take a look at King Solomon.

Wisdom That Matters

Solomon, the son of King David, was considered to have had God's wisdom bestowed upon him. Kings and leaders came from around the world to seek out this highly regarded wisdom. And as a result, God made him the builder of His first non-tent temple. King Solomon grew to such incredible wealth and success, that it has been said he was the wealthiest man in the world. And he himself tells us that he had riches in all forms such as to make any earthly palace pale in comparison to Solomon's wealth. His list in Ecclesiastes 2 is long and one we are tempted to envy, and yet, Solomon felt empty in his later years. He had it all. He was the walking definition of what it meant to have it all.

Solomon himself said, "If something appealed to me, I did it. I allowed myself to have any pleasure I wanted, since I found pleasure in my work." (Ecclesiastes 2:10) However, in verse 11 Solomon follows that comment with, "But when I turned to look at all that I had accomplished and all the hard work I had put into it, I saw it was all pointless. [It was like] trying to catch the wind. I gained nothing."

Why did Solomon call all that he accomplished the "vanity of vanities?" Even worse, he said he "came to hate life." Because Solomon had gotten off track along the way and if you look back at his list of lists in Ecclesiastes 2:4-10, you'll see he worked for one person, himself. He forgot that his work was supposed be his worship to his Lord. He forgot to keep God as his CEO. "It is a gift from God to be able to...experience the good that comes from every kind of hard work. I realize that whatever God does will last forever. Nothing can be added to it, and nothing can be taken away from it. God does this so people will fear Him." (Ecclesiastes 3:13-14) Solomon's great achievements alone couldn't provide the purpose, satisfaction, and significance he desired. Nonetheless Solomon knew and acknowledged that work and the ability to see good in work, is a gift from God, and no one can find satisfaction or enjoyment without Him. (Ecclesiastes 2)

When your work is your worship, it can all be made for good and enjoyed. But when your work does not involve God, any accomplishment you create, no matter how opulent or grand, will be the "vanity of vanities." So, in order to not suffer this vacuous disappointment, we must first keep it clear that God is our sole reason for our work. He is the reason we start a business. He is the only definition behind our business.

A Kingdom Business is not merely defined by a business that gives its profits to God's mission or a business that works with ethical standards. A Kingdom Business stands distinct from other business in five specific spiritual ways. Let's look to Ephesians 6 for those critical distinctions.

The Five Distinctions of Kingdom Business

Take a look at Ephesians 6, and think about your business as you read it. As a Christ follower, you may agree with the concept of work as worship, but you might ask, "What does that mean for my work? How does it change how I approach running my company?"

But before we look at these passages, starting at verse five, please take into account that this letter was written two thousand years ago in a radically different cultural context. So, let's be clear that God hates slavery. He abhors it! When you read Paul's letter to Timothy, you learn that slavery is at the top of the list of things that God absolutely hates. He has hated slavery throughout human history and He hates it today with almost 30 million slaves in our world.

Now picture this New Testament church of 40 or 50 men, sitting in a room together both masters and slaves, side-by-side. This was completely counter-cultural. It was unheard of that masters and slaves would gather together to listen to the instructions of this letter, written to them by Paul. Paul was clear and direct in telling them how they should work and what that work unto God should be like. In this ancient business meeting, we have the various sectors of the economic workforce. From Paul's instructions to them we can draw the distinctions God has created for Kingdom Business.

Starting in verse five: "Slaves, obey your earthly masters with respect and fear, and with sincerity of heart, just as you would obey Christ. 6 Obey them not only to win their favor when their eye is on you, but as slaves of Christ, doing the will of God from your heart. 7 Serve wholeheartedly, as if you were serving the Lord, not people, 8 because you know that the Lord will reward each one for whatever good they do, whether they are slave or free. 9 And masters, treat your slaves in the same way. Do not threaten them, since you know that he who is both their Master and yours is in heaven, and there is no favoritism with him."

These five verses give five distinctions for Kingdom Business:

1. Christ is your CEO. (v. 5)
2. Work is your calling. (v. 6)
3. The Holy Spirit is your CSO. (v. 7)
4. Your rewards come from God. (v. 8)
5. People are the priority. (v. 9)

Christ is Your CEO

Paul says if you are going to work, work just as if you would obey Christ. If work is worship, than Christ is my CEO and serving Him is my motivation. We see Christ as our Savior, our healer, our counselor, as a boss over our morals, maybe even as a boss over our money, but Christ as our workplace boss? When you read the book of Genesis, you discover that God created work even before He created family. Don't misunderstand me. Family is very important, but work, especially as a family, is also very important. Kingdom Business is distinct because its foundation is rooted in God as the real true Boss of the business.

I will give you a little bit of insight into my life. I have never really had a boss like most people. Never. When I was in a university, I worked my way through college buying and selling stuff. It was before Christian values took root into my life so I would buy stuff cheap and sell it for a much higher price. When I served in church I was the lead pastor, so although the church had a board, I didn't really have a boss managing my daily work. I didn't punch a clock. For the past 15 years I have been self-employed, consulting with churches, business and civic organizations – again, no boss. I have never had a boss.

When people hear that I have gone through all of my life without a boss, they become greatly jealous. They think, "Wow, wouldn't it be great not to have a boss?" Society values having no boss. But "no boss" is actually the opposite of God's design.

If work is worship then you recognize that ultimately Christ is your CEO. How you work is living out His image through your work. Let that sink in. Re-read it if you need. With Christ as your boss, your business becomes your offering to Him. MLK Jr. put it best when he said, "If a man is called to be a street sweeper, he should sweep streets just as Michelangelo painted or Beethoven composed music, or Shakespeare wrote poetry. He should sweep streets so well that all the hosts of heaven and earth will pause to say, "Here lived a great street sweeper who did his job well." Work as worship.

Can you imagine having a better boss? 85% of people quit their jobs because of having a less than stellar boss. But having Christ as your CEO means you have the sharpest mind for your business. Your boss is the guy who created the idea of business. Talk about having an inside track on strategic wisdom. You thought Solomon was wise. Imagine having the greatest mind ever working your business as the CEO.

This is Your Calling

Look at the second distinguishing concept, found in verse six. Paul says that when you are working it is to be that you are doing the will of God from your heart. We are to work from a deep desire to do what God wants us to do. If work is worship, then my calling can be found in my work. Now we have a dilemma with this because we have the tendency to take life and put it into two separate categories called the sacred and the secular. These are nice neat boxes aren't they? The sacred is what I do that seems spiritual: I go to church. I read my bible. I pray. The secular is what I do that doesn't seem very sacred and work is at the front of the line of what doesn't look very sacred. At work I have to deal with nasty people. I see corrupt practices. I don't go to work and read my Bible like a pastor does. I can't even listen to worship music. Surely, work can't be sacred.

We have these two boxes that compartmentalize the sacred and the secular. The government reinforces this separation as it tells us that we can have our religion, but only as long as we keep it private. Do not bring it into the public forum, we are told. The marketplace reinforces this separation because some businesses do not have much that is sacred about their practice whatsoever. There is a lot of ungodliness that goes on in business. The church even reinforces this separation. It says if you are going to go into ministry, become a pastor and work in a church. If you can't, then make sure you pray and support those that do.

Let me ask you a question. Are you a fulltime minister? You say, "No Joel, I'm a business owner, remember." At the risk of seeming redundant or coy, let me ask you again. Are you a fulltime minister? What if I told you that that God says you are a fulltime minister.

Here is God's strategy. Think about it, what is the best way to reach a young student? God knows how. He takes a fulltime minister, gives her good brains and a lot of patience and then sneakily has her start her own private school. He is so crafty this way as she gets to live out her calling through her work. What about a construction worker? Again, God takes a fulltime minister, a construction company foreman/owner, perhaps with some bold tattoos and puts him on a construction project with construction workers. Construction workers may never listen to a pastor, so God in His sneaky way, puts the fulltime minister in the middle of these construction workers. This fulltime minister shows how to work with integrity and build the best home possible. He is fulfilling his calling to God in running his construction business.

So, now let's visit the question again, but this time, you know the answer. I'll help you here. You are in fulltime ministry. If you see your business as joining God in healing communities and do it unto the Lord with your heart, it stops being toil and becomes worship. Without your heart, there is no calling in it. Please understand that you didn't start out as a school owner or construction company owner, you started out as a fulltime minister. God just wired you and slotted you rather stealthily in your work, where you would be happy and where His Kingdom would flourish because of you. However, in the next principle, we will see that it will take even more than just what your heart can bring. You'll need a CSO.

Trust Your CSO

The third principle found in verse seven says you must serve eagerly or wholeheartedly. Here's where you may ask almost incredulously, "I can barely drag my heavily caffeinated, lackluster body in each day to deal with all the myriad of challenges that await me and you want me to bring my whole heart? The idea of serving wholeheartedly is that you are to trust fully in your heart, the direction God leads you in your work and business. How do you do that? Make the Holy Spirit your CSO. What is a CSO? The CEO is the Chief Executive Officer, the CFO is the Chief Financial Officer, and a CSO is the Chief Strategy Officer.

If you are going operate a Kingdom Business, then you must be fully committed to what God wants you to do. But more than that, you need to allow Him to lead and direct your business. Kingdom Business uses the best practices possible, but never trumps natural strategies over the leading of the Holy Spirit. This may sound super-spiritual but here's the good news, not only has God "got your back," but His Holy Spirit joins you to add to your knowledge any and all wisdom that you may lack. (2 Corinthians 12:9-10)

It is interesting that when we read the scriptures, we know that God wants to be worshiped. But then God goes on to tell us *how* He wants to be worshiped. He is in fact, quite specific about it. He tells us the kind of instruments He wants us to use in worshiping Him. He tells us when and how He wants us to worship, and one of the lines He uses in describing worshiping is that you must worship "in spirit and in truth." It is like He is saying, "Hey listen, don't think that you can operate a business with just your own energy. Do not think that you can go in there and worship Me knowing the challenges and people you have to face. You are going to need something supernatural breathed into you, My Spirit."

So if work is worship, before I go into work tomorrow I will say to myself, "Holy Spirit, fill me because there are issues I'm not able to tackle without You. If I am going to worship you, I need peace at my work, but I can't conjure up the peace I need with my own energy." God, by His Spirit, will come down and breathe peace into you. Now you can go into your work place with a peace that "passes all understanding." This is a peace that only He can give you. Some of you go into work environments where you most definitely need compassion for people that are hard to work with, people who will betray you. First you pray, "Holy Spirit, fill me." And He breathes compassion into you. You also need an authority to lead with respect and devotion. The Holy Spirit fills you with conviction and an authority from God that enables you to be a strong leader.

Please be aware, there will be times when you will be counter-cultural if you do trust the leading of the Holy Spirit. While business leaders all around you are cutting corners to increase their margins you must say to yourself, "I am not going to cut corners that negatively affect my employees or clientele simply to drive profits. Why? Because the Spirit of God fills me and allows me to lead and be guided by serving whole-heartedly what the Holy Spirit asks of me." Sometimes the Holy Spirit gives you creative entrepreneurial ideas for business that seem contrary to conventional wisdom. Although these times are rare, don't disregard them.

Listen to Him, because God is watching and maneuvering and positioning you to cause your business to flourish. Following His leading is a true act of worship to Him. I had this so clearly illustrated to me a few years ago. I had traveled three thousand miles from my home in Chicago to speak at a church in Los Angeles. It was a large church with numerous Sunday services. I had completed four of the five services and was resting in the pastor's office between services. Suddenly I got this impression in my heart to call home. I thought, "That's kind of silly. I travel often away from home and I've never had an impression to call home." But undeniably the impression was so strong - Call home. So I called my wife. Nobody answered, which was a little unusual. I thought, "That's kind of strange, but no big deal." Again the impression...Call home! So I called my daughter who answered her phone and immediately told me to "Call Mom." Something has happened.

I called my wife a third time and this time she answered. She explained how she had picked up our son from church camp, where the day before, his appendix had burst and he was in severe pain with an internal rupture. She had rushed him to the emergency room where they were preparing to take him into emergency surgery. I hung up the phone with the only goal of getting home as soon as possible. But I had another service left to preach, and my flight wasn't until 10:00PM that night. I knew what a madhouse LAX can be. A staff pastor willingly preached the final service for me while yet another pastor drove me quickly to the airport.

I really didn't know what I was going to do. "How on earth am I going to get home in time?" I walked into LAX and all I could see were people everywhere. The security line was so long, every counter had a long line of people and I knew just standing in a long line would not get me home. So I walked towards the end of a counter where there were no people, with no options in my mind. Now watch, here is where God is working. He sees one of His children needing help. So He takes another one of his children and moves her exactly where she is needed so she will be able to help. But this only happens if that child is at work, listening to the Holy Spirit because her work is worship. This is what happened to me.

I am standing at the end of the counter and begin to pray because I need to get home to my son and my wife and don't have the ability to do this. Suddenly a representative of the airline I'm flying with approaches me to ask if she can help. Think of it, an airline employee initiating help? This is the complete truth. I quickly explain my predicament. I tell her, "My son is going into emergency surgery and I need to get home. I don't know what to do." She says, "Come with me," and walks me over to a computer terminal. She inputs some data and prints out a boarding pass.

She doesn't hand me the board pass however. She instructs me, "Follow me." She walks me through security to the front of the line where everyone glares angrily not knowing how I got special treatment to cut in the front of the line. Once through security she quickly walks me right up to my gate just before it closes. I am able to get on the flight and as I walk through the door I turn around and say to her my most heart-felt, "Thank you!"

This is where the story gets really good. She replies to me, "I'll pray for your son." Right then, I knew that she was a Christ follower and that she saw the Holy Spirit as her Chief Strategy Officer. She was following His leading every step of the way. I am so grateful that her day at work was not just another day as usual. That she saw her work as worship and thus had her spiritual antennas up, waiting and expecting God to lead her.

Thinking about it later, I thought how pleased God must have been, looking down saying to angels nearby, "Did you see that lady worship Me?" He was so honored in the worship that one of his children gave to Him through her work. When you meet with your employees or clients, how will you lead them? Will business be just about looking at profit margins only, or will you say, "Wow Lord, this is my worship to you! You are my boss and here is my calling. You have wired me for this, but Holy Spirit, I need you. Lead me today in all that I do because with you Holy Spirit, my work will simply be human effort." Your Kingdom Calling is not to engage in business through human effort alone. God calls you and then He graces you with His daily presence and leadership through His Holy Spirit.

Kingdom ROI (Return on Investment)

On to the fourth principle. Look at verse eight. In verse eight, it says the Lord rewards each one, for whatever good he or she does. If your business is a Kingdom Business, then you will see God as the true source of all your rewards. He is the one that pays you, leads you, paves the way for you and ultimately determines the fate of your company. Let's look deeper into this.

Let's look at a common misconception. We believe our profits are dependent in one way or another on other people. We are in a business; if the business flourishes then we make money. Our business is part of a larger industry. If that industry is not flourishing, our profits are negatively affected by the industry. Our business, and the industry it represents are part of a greater overall economy, which ultimately affects our business. When we think of our reward, we base it upon the people we work with, the business we lead, the industry of which it is a part and the economy in which the business functions. It seems our reward is contingent on so many variables over which we have little or no control.

That is how most of us see the return on investment in our business. But God gives us an amazing promise. He says, "No, if your work is worship and you're serving for Me, I will reward each one of you for the good you have done." There is a tremendous promise and a unique distinction for Kingdom Business. Your return on investment (your reward) is not solely linked to your clientele, it is not reliant upon your business production. It is not even truly dependent on the industry or economy. You can have a confidence that says, "God is my source, He is my boss, He is the one who will provide for me. So I am going to trust Him with this." There is a promise that says God provides your reward. He is the one who "pays you," and here's how.

There are three different ways that God rewards us based upon how we worship Him with our work. First He rewards us materially. We get a paycheck. What is of utmost importance here is that if work is worship, when I get that paycheck, I am to see God as my source for that paycheck. Let's be honest, when we get that check, often times the first thing we think is, "I wish it was a little bigger." But there is more going on than just the paycheck. This is really an issue of contentment and too narrow a view of how God rewards.

I was talking to a Christian construction firm owner who was finishing up building a house. He mentioned that his client was going to be paying him for the job. He hadn't yet seen how God was a part of this entire business process. I asked him what he used to build the house. He identified lumber, hardware and other raw materials, which I pointed out to him God had provided through creation. Suddenly the light of truth went on for him. He realized that God had given him raw materials, which he stewarded to build a house. He then understood that although the payment came from the client, it actually was God who had rewarded him.

God really is the one true source. God is the source of your income, and when you know that, there is contentment and gratitude as you realize there is a bigger story going on with your business. Whenever you wish you were getting paid more, realize that God rewards in other ways with far greater benefit than just money.

Second, God rewards us internally as our character changes, grows, and matures. When we go into work with our work as worship, and we live out our Christ calling, something inside begins to change. The airline representative that had worshiped God by helping me had the sweet reward of knowing that she had served a family. I am confident that the rest of her day was elevated by that beautiful act of worship. Her character grew. Christ in her grew. This is spiritual formation. I hope you recognize that the character and identity of Christ being formed in you will always trump money. Could we begin to see the monetary reward as the byproduct and the internal benefits as the main reward?

This internal character of Christ formation has many benefits that come with it. When I graduated from college I worked with gangs in Chicago. It was rough work and I didn't get paid very much. But while I was working with these gang bangers, I grew in my Christ-like character, which for me was far more valuable than money. Compassion grew in me, wisdom grew in me, and the fruit of the Spirit grew in me. Inside I changed. As a result, I was attracting something more valuable than money, something God calls worth more than rubies. I was attracting my future wife.

At the time I'm describing, there was this single lady named Marie in my church - our church, I guess. On the outside, I don't have much to attract a lady. No six pack abs. No wavy hair or dreamy blue eyes. But Marie saw something inside me that was very attractive to her. I was smokin' hot on the inside. Character was growing and she wanted to get to know this guy. I am now a very rich man, because God gave her to me as my wife. Sure, He rewards us materially, but He also rewards us internally so we can become someone more like Jesus.

And finally God rewards us eternally. This is the part that is a little mysterious because none of us quite know what that reward truly looks like. There are some pictures of gold streets and amazing mansions but no one has ever been there and then reported back to us in earthly detail on God's eternal reward system. This eternal reward demands a measure of faith on our part.

If I treat work as worship, Christ is my boss. This is where my calling can be. The Holy Spirit fills me and my source is God. He will take care of me materially. He will grow in me and if that wasn't enough, on the other side of heaven, there will be reward for me that I cannot even imagine. I have faith that it is waiting for me. It's like signing an employee contract without fully knowing the remuneration you'll receive. Most contracts have specific stipulations regarding the company's expectations for your work and how they will pay you. You read the contract carefully before signing it. But with God, it's as if He gives you a contract that is blank. He simply asks you to trust Him and sign it, without fully knowing your complete reward. Kingdom Business is distinct as we accept that a portion of our return on our investment will not be known until eternity. We do business, by faith.

Marie and I have a friend who started a company on the south side of Chicago in one of the city's worst neighborhoods. This community has 50% unemployment and most of the young men end up in prison. Our friend imports tea that he packages and then sells to restaurants. But he is very intentional with his business because his work is worship. He doesn't see his business simply as a profit-making venture through the sale of tea.

He intentionally hires young men, often high school dropouts. On their first day he explains to them, "Listen, I am only want you working here for three or four years. I do not want you to stay in this factory any longer. Here is what I'm going to do. You work for us and we will make sure you achieve your next level of education, whether it's a high school diploma, college degree or trade certification. You tell me what you want to do with your life. Tell me what your dream is and while you're working here, I will give you, during the next three or four years, the opportunity to achieve that dream and get into the career you want. My friend hires these young men who otherwise have no opportunity because society has discarded them. He mentors and educates them. He realizes that his business could make more financial profit with less employee turnover but he knows that God rewards him, not just materially but eternally. Sure, his company prospers financially, but he also knows he will grow in character and even beyond that, there is a reward the other side of Heaven for him as his work is worship.

What about you? How will you see your business? It will either be toil and drudgery or it will be a reflection of your Kingdom Calling, that proclaims, "God I get a chance to serve you and I get a chance to worship You in a way that I otherwise would never have. I get a chance to partner with You to heal communities while I live out your purpose for me."

Every Life Has Equal Value

Here is the last of the five principles from Ephesians six. Look at the last verse. Paul made a very powerful statement two thousand years ago that still needs to be made today. He said, "Remember, with the Lord there is no favoritism." Notice, there are masters and slaves listening to this. And they are surely thinking, "Wow, no favoritism? Every life has equal value?" What Paul was indicating and what the Holy Spirit is telling us in Paul's recorded words, is that when work is worship, then people are the priority. There is no favoritism. Every life has equal value. Now that's a counter-cultural thought for business!

If we're honest, in most business operations, favoritism with people is at the core of how business is done. We can so easily get caught up in a need to advance the business that we cozy up to only the individuals that can make us more successful, falling to the temptation to show favoritism. We do this in maneuvering for promotions. We do this is leveraging our staff. We do this with vendors and clients. Paul says, "No, in the Kingdom there is no favoritism." The janitor is no less valuable than the Executive Vice-President of Finance. Who do you invite to the company Christmas party or share your box seats with? If work is worship then Paul makes it abundantly clear, people are the priority. No favoritism. You have to walk into work and say, "Okay God, give me your eyes with which to view everyone here so that I can be a light for You." The best way your business will embody this Kingdom distinction is through integrity. Here is why.

When you have Christ-like integrity, that character leads to conversations. Conversations lead to conversions where God can be the true Author of healing. We get caught up in conversions. We measure our work for God by conversions. Don't worry about conversions, but count the conversations. Let me repeat that, count the conversations not the conversions. Conversations begin with integrity. Conversations, meaningful ones, with employees, clients and vendors, take place because of your character.

I was coming to church one Sunday morning. I was driving into the parking lot following a car with a husband and wife inside. It was obvious that they were fighting. They were pointing fingers at each other and although their windows were rolled up so they couldn't be heard, they were definitely yelling at each other. They pulled into a parking spot, so I parked three spots over afraid the fight would spill out into the parking lot. But then the funniest thing happened. The moment they stepped out of their car, everything changed. They put these fake smiles on their faces. They gently shut the car door and proceed to hold hands while walking into the church. I was walking behind them laughing, but thinking to myself, "You can fool people for an hour and a half in church, but you cannot fool people eight hours a day at your workplace." Character really counts.

Here is what character is. Take your convictions, what you really believe. Then take what you say, and your actions, how you truly live, and see if the three: convictions, words and actions, line up. If they do, you have character. My words, my actions and what I believe, my convictions, must be in complete harmony to operate in Godly character. As long as those three line up, then I am going to be living out Christ-like character. Many of you work in places where these three are not aligned. People say things but they do not act accordingly. People say things that they don't actually believe. But as Christ followers, God says to us, "Listen, you have character, you have what you believe, what you know is true, and you've got your words. What you believe and how you speak and live need to line up." With that kind of Christ-like character the world sees your good deeds that reflect to your Father in Heaven.

People will notice something very different about you. Christ-like character is what leads to conversations that you don't even need to initiate. People will see your company as one that is trustworthy and can deliver on its promise. They may not even be sure why, but it's your company that wins the bid. Something about you just seems right. They will call you when they have a choice of businesses. Your employees will honor you because they know they can trust you. Your vendors will give you the best deals because they know this partnership will be long-term. God can and will bless your business regardless of worldly factors if you are operating a Kingdom Business. And your integrity will result in a witness to the character and love of God.

There are many businesses in this world. All want to be profitable, but not all are Kingdom Business. When God is your CEO, when you know your work is your calling, when the Holy Spirit is your CSO, when you know your reward comes from heaven and when there is no favoritism because every person has equal value, then you have a Kingdom Business.

Questions

1. What does it look like when you make the Lord your CEO and CSO?

2. Which form of ROI from God has been your primary way of seeing His reward? How do the three ways He profits you affect how you see your business?

3. How can you better align your Christ-like character as a business leader in His Kingdom?

Chapter Three

Building a Kingdom Business

"And as for you, be fruitful and multiply. Bring forth abundantly in the earth and multiply in it."

As you've now read so far, from the very beginning God created us to co-create and prosper with all that He gave us on this earth. And when we do so, we are to reflect Him so the world can see Him through us. This Creation Mandate, God clearly felt was so critical to His plan of prosperity and peace for us, that when we couldn't get it right more than once throughout history, He sent His Son to redeem us and redeem work. Now when we walk in His plan for us, work is meant to be and can be an act of worship to Him, especially when our work or business lines up with the five distinctions we covered in chapter two.

Now let's take it even a step further.

The subtitle to this book best introduces this chapter: Harnessing the power of business to transform the world. Changing the world through work is not just about the role of the individual. Changing the world is also about the role of the institution of business. It is not just what you should do but it is what a business should look like and how it should function to transform its community. Just as we define what the church should look like, apart from the pastor, we should also define what a Kingdom business should look like, apart from the owner. What's key is how a business should operate as a profit-making institution and not as a charity. Therefore, as a result of my business consulting experience especially in the last few years, I want to help you navigate these exciting waters and get the most possible out of the adventure.

How should you go about building a Kingdom Business that will fulfill God's Creation Mandate and pay you and all affected by the business with rewards financial, internal and eternal? I want your business to see growth you never anticipated while you see communities flourish through your work as worship to God.

I also want to help you avoid possible pitfalls I've seen other companies struggle by engaging in worthy endeavors yet they found their business hurt by this "mission work." Your business is perfectly equipped to transform your community when it is a Kingdom Business. So let's get to it.

What's Your Role?

There is an African parable that tells of four women that come upon a section of the river where babies are drowning. The first woman jumps in immediately and furiously tries to save as many babies as she can. The second works to teach the babies how to swim. The third woman walks upstream to figure out where, how, and why these babies are getting into the river. And the fourth woman goes back to the village to study to see if this has happened any place else and what can be learned from it.

The lesson of the parable is that each of these women had a role in improving the situation, each role equally needed and valuable. However, the message for your company as you (and all involved) build a Kingdom Business is that you need to look at what role God has designed you to play in His Creation Mandate. If you want a true Kingdom Business that in its very identity is God's work, then take some time and some intentionality to relook at the role of your business in God's Kingdom.

In fact, it is important to keep a sense of perspective here. The Bible talks about many parts of the body each with its own gifts being equally valuable. Think your pinky toe doesn't matter? Talk to someone that had to learn to walk without it. You are meant to operate in your business identity and only that, because frankly that is all you'll be good at and it's more than enough. Just like the Church is built up of thousands of churches with different flavors, personalities and styles, your business is meant to join thousands of other businesses in God's Creation Mandate. Your business plays a key role, but only the role that it was meant for, not some other business's role. Furthermore, don't underestimate the effect of the business' one role. You have no idea the incredible ripple effect one small act can create when it's laid at God's feet. One business provides a backyard garden service, creating healthy, ready to pick off the vine vegetables. This business is bringing health and comfort to families. Be secure in that one role, knowing you are part of a Kingdom Business, and it's a big Kingdom with lots of businesses, all doing their part.

That being said, my experience tells me that perhaps as you get your feet deeper into these waters, you'll want to deepen your very business identity, lead other businesses to follow in the trail you are blazing, provide a rich, meaningful work experience for your employees, and have a business that blends both its work (it's product or service) with its creative initiatives all to the Glory of God for the benefit of all involved. To do that, consider applying the principles I set out in this chapter. Also embrace my warnings from businesses, with well-intentioned leaders, who have encountered serious pitfalls all in the name of God's Kingdom work. To begin building a Kingdom Business, like everything else in God's Kingdom, you must start on the inside. You must start with the heart of the business.

What's Your Motivation?

Motivation is very different than role, so please don't mistake the two. Your role is fitting into the custom mold that God created just for you, like a good lounge chair. Motivation, on the other hand is the big why in the sky. Knowing the right motivation directly correlates to the fruitfulness your business will have for God's Kingdom. It will be fruitful, because God is in charge. But whether it has 30-fold fruit or 100-fold fruit is due in part to the motivation of your heart as the leader.

I know we are talking about business as an institution, but the big why in the sky begins with your personal relationship with Christ.

It is a very natural outgrowth of walking in God's plan of abundance, that we will be moved to do even more for His Kingdom through our work calling. There are multiple places in the Bible that make it evident that we will be moved to do good works not in any way to be saved, but rather as an expression of our love and gratitude to Him and as a result of the Holy Spirit dwelling in us after salvation. In fact, Ephesians 2:10 says that while Christ's work made us a new creation in God's eyes, it was done in part so that we could do the "good works" that God prepared for us ahead of time. James even went so far as to say that our "faith without works is dead." This isn't just because our faith isn't real if we don't act on it, but because our faith doesn't help others if we just say, "God bless you," but don't do anything to reflect God's love by doing something to bless those in need of His love. (James 2:14-17)

Look at it on an individual level, when you were courting your spouse (and hopefully you still court your spouse years down the line), weren't you just giddy to show even the most ridiculous acts of love like flowers, jewelry, tickets to monster truck rallies? No one really needs any of those things, but we naturally express our love in acts. It's the same with your Kingdom Business.

I say all this simply to lead up to my main point heading into this chapter. I want to make it crystal clear in your mind that you already have a Kingdom Business if you operate in the Creation Mandate and the distinctions we covered in Ephesians six. If you are a sign maker and you make God your CEO and CSO and you make really good signs that serve the public's needs, you're there. You're doing it; you have a Kingdom Business!

Understand that a business is a Kingdom Business by the very nature of its identity and purpose. A software development company that funds feeding programs with a portion of its profits is a caring business. But a software development company that develops software for restaurants to account for unsold food, avoiding waste, and resulting in an efficient distribution of leftovers to soup kitchens – that is Kingdom Business. It is a very profitable business that is fulfilling God's Creation Mandate.

But, don't be surprised that God may call your heart to do more, for society's benefit. Don't be surprised that God has community transformation projects already laid out for you through your business. These community projects are not the ministry side of your business. Your business is Kingdom. Nor are these community projects a requirement of being a Kingdom Business. Your business is Kingdom. However, your Kingdom business vision will grow to have projects – in line with your calling – that will have a more explicit community service. These projects will help define your business as more than a profit-making endeavor.

My hope is that your why will be a natural outgrowth of the success of your business, thus affording you the opportunity to do projects that reflect God's love for a community. You see, I've observed many companies take on a profile of wanting to transform its community, but without the right motivation, the end result is not greatly productive. I've categorized businesses that are harnessing their power to transform their community into what I call the Five Levels of Motivation. None are bad but only one is truly Kingdom-centered.

The first level of motivation is Compliance. Here companies are motivated to set up policies to be in compliance so they can continue making profits, but there is no true care, especially for their workforce. A great example of this is the outsourcing of labor to developing countries where labor is cheap. International companies, working with local businesses often create very unsafe environments where workers are injured and even die. In response to new regulations, companies will post safety signs for workers, telling them of their rights in the workplace. However, the signs put up in compliance with building codes and rights of workers, are posted in English and none of the workers read English. No real care in the action.

The next level of motivation is Promotional. Companies make necessary infrastructure changes such as "going green" which are often seen as responsible but these changes are made, not from a value base but predominantly as a PR benefit. "What could we do that would make our community hold us in a higher regard?" is the question this motivation answers. It is not core to their identity, but rather seen as a necessary cost to look good to the companies clientele.

The third level of motivation is Activity. Companies want to do something good, usually in response to the prodding of their employees or to requests from the community. However the projects taken on have little or no relevance to the business identity and practice. The company fulfills a random list of ad hoc initiatives, but with no connection to its company identity and purpose. The motivation may be to do good, but the activity is not viewed as an integral part of the business' mission.

Similar, but a little more in line with core company identity, is the fourth motivation that I've labeled as Strategic. An example of this is car companies now producing hybrid vehicles. Making cars is the identity of the company so their "community" work is in line with their business mission. Thus they help the environment using their core competencies. There is no compartmentalization between their community work and their profit-making business. However, if hybrid-cars were not profitable, the companies would quickly suspend their production. The community transformation is done as a result of a cost benefit analysis that determines greater profits. The motivation is driven by what's best for the business.

The fifth and final motivation – the one that comes straight from the heart of God for harnessing the power of business to transform the world is what I call, Kingdom Called. This is where the company is operating out of its very core identity seeking to make the community and the world a better place. Kingdom Called is when a company desires to do a great thing that helps others, as part of their mission, even involving vendors and the public, building partnerships and creating more layers of profit that can be imagined.

The company serves its community, not just from a PR study or due to criticism or compliance, not because it brings client allegiance or huge profits (though all these factors will likely come into play), but because the company is uniquely able and wants to transform the world for the better. Google's recent initiative to eradicate child porn from the Internet is an example of this. This company allocated millions of dollars and partnered with Microsoft to help create technology that "even its rivals can use," according to the Huffington Post. Whether Google is aware of it or not, and whether they give glory to God or not, their motivation comes from His Kingdom heart. You don't think God is going to smile on this initiative in ways big and small that we may never even hear about, far beyond rising stock? Guaranteed.

Its important to recognize that motivation does not stand in conflict with profit making. You don't have to lose money in order to have a pure motivation. Motivation is a condition of the heart. Owners, board members and even employees always need to keep their heart pure before the Lord so that when profits and margins increase, the motivation stays true. One business I consulted with, saw this very thing happen. As they began to increase their community projects their business reputation grew. Like TOMS, this business is seen as genuinely caring about the community, because well... they genuinely care about the community. This created a tension however for the leadership of the business. They were grateful for the increased positive public awareness for their business but they were hesitant because they didn't take on the community projects for their marketing value. If your business is going to have influence, it will not remain the world's best-kept secret. But when the secret gets out, you will always need to monitor your motivation so that your work remains true to its Kingdom Calling. You will always have a tension between doing good things for God in your community from a pure motivation, and seeing those good works greatly benefit the business. I told this business that as long as there was tension, they were in a good place.

Beyond Motivation – Building a Kingdom Business

To build a Kingdom Business you must start with your motivation but a good heart alone won't result in the most effective and profitable business. Once you've set the foundation of your heart, you need to move forward and build a Kingdom Business. Here's the irony. If you're already building your business and your business itself is Kingdom, then why do you need to build something more for it to be Kingdom Business? You don't. Here's the catch. As you own a business that is working well you've already got various strategic components, like vision, organizational design, personnel and operational strategies working for you. The key is not to change what you have nor is it to create a second strategy, separate from your business. So what do you do? You take what God has already built, but you advance it to better represent the Kingdom Business you are discovering. You do this in three areas:

1. The Identity of the business, in terms of its Kingdom Calling
2. The Involvement of the people, connected to the business
3. The Initiatives of the business in the community, which enhance your business' Kingdom profile

Identity of the Business

Your business has an identity and a purpose. But, like most companies, the mission of the business is rooted in language around its bottom line or its project operations, not the advancement of the community.   Don't make the mistake of creating a second mission representing your business' community work. Wrong move. Remember your business is not designed to be a missions ministry. Your business is mission. What you need to do is identify how your current business is helping its community. The biggest challenge I've experienced in consulting with businesses is that they quickly define their mission vision by a community project to be completed.

You need foremost to keep your Kingdom identity integrated into your business, your values, and your practices.   The challenge is that your business identity needs to speak to an audience that is not necessarily Christian.   One company, rebranded their mission statement to "Making Better Lives in the City of Tomorrow".   The owners clearly knew their vision was rooted in Jeremiah 29 and God's charge to Israel to "seek the peace of the city to which I have called you, by building homes there," but they found language that would speak to a broader audience. One vision. One identity. It is critically important that you operate within your business identity and stay true to that identity to be most effective. You need to truly know what God has called your business to be. Don't make community transformation a bolt-on charity that your business funds but which functions separate from your business. That's a charity, not a Kingdom Business.

One business, working to integrate its mission with its identity, slightly altered their weekly operational updates. Now each project team had to include in their update how the project was affecting the lives of people, not just the fulfillment of the project deadlines. At first it was awkward and seemed forced, but over weeks, a sense of purpose took place.   Work began to be more centered on community flourishing than just the project. Their language began to affect their work. The Kingdom business identity began to take hold.

Involvement of People

Please remember the business vision is not only about you. Sure, you may be the President or head of your company, but collaboration is critical, especially if you want to see changed lives. People will be a part of something they have helped to create. And if people have helped to create it, it will transform them. Your projects are about your company's identity, its culture and its values. Your management and your employees should be in on the planning and generating of ideas. I have even worked with a Kingdom Businesses that used client input to help generate its project vision. Stay authentic to your calling and competency, but collaborate to build ownership and commitment for greater benefit to all involved.

I know this is not a new concept, but it's easy to get wrapped up in thinking that we as leaders should drive the machine, and to some degree we should, but it's good to have input since this will touch many lives. You can use your vision for transforming the world to educate people on your company identity and core competencies. You can engage your team to see what is important to each of them; see where their strengths may lie within the company identity. Who knows, you may have connections and skills at your fingertips of which you were completely unaware.

One company I consulted had 120 employees. They discovered 10-12 employees who were very passionate about helping their community. Simply as a starting point, they empowered this team to identify opportunities locally that would reflect the vision of the company, even if the projects weren't financially profitable. They developed a communication strategy for keeping the business "talking" about the good happening through its work. And by the "business," I mean the people. Some businesses use a monthly newsletter. Others provide updates at staff gatherings. Whatever your way of engaging people, remember that vision leaks. Harnessing the power of business to change the world is a thought that needs to be continually put in front of your team.

With your employees, decide what kind of training, communication and even morale building will be needed. One company I work with generates a monthly e-news that updates all its profitable projects in light of the impact being felt by people, the enhancement being brought to the community. They've created a separate twitter account for the business that focuses solely on how the business is changing the world. Clients, vendors, employees and any interested party can follow this account. Its one way they are setting a culture and identity for their business..

Besides your employees, as your Kingdom vision progresses, God will give you the opportunity to engage with your vendors and other businesses as partners in your community transformation work. One business asked all its vendors to contribute to an orphanage project in Africa in lieu of the typical Christmas gifts normally given by the vendors. The vendors were so inspired that one vendor (who was not a Christian) even travelled to Africa to serve the children on a short-term trip. There will likely be other businesses you know that have a skill or product that is part of their core competency, so why waste energy and resources trying to do everything? When the time is right, invite other businesses into partnerships for community transformation.

In all these relationship-building opportunities, go with a spirit of unity. Respect is paramount. Nurture the relationships through stages; make time and financial investments into these relationships. People matter.

Initiatives in the Community

Ever heard the saying, "Don't try to be someone else, that part is already taken." Ever seen a girl 4'8" playing volleyball or basketball? Ever seen a girl 6'4" tall do gymnastics? Hey, "all things are possible through Christ who strengthens me" but unless God has made a point to communicate something uniquely special to you, stick with your strengths and identity as a business. If you're a sign maker, your community projects should be a natural extension of the Kingdom work your business does. I knew a sign-making business that provided welcome signs for a special banquet for homeless people. The signs were a great inspiration and set the tone for the dinner and the relationships that would come out of that evening.

What seemed like a small, insignificant work, was actually "harnessing the power of business to transform the world", because God works best through our seemingly small insignificant works. The sign-making business was integral to God's ministry and used by Him to heal lives. Your business must integrate its identity and work or chances are it will try to be something and do something God had earmarked for another business. Vision for your business to change the world must remain true to the business identity and competency.

It is also important to stay open to doors of opportunities that you may not be aware of. One company discovered that its city had become one of the "host towns" for the Special Olympic athletes an upcoming Special Olympics. And one of their clients was connected with city officials so he was knew all the plans and opportunities to serve these athletes and their families leading up to their competition. This company's industry was committed to family and determined this opportunity fit their corporate vision. Their motivation was pure. Their vision was integrated with the business. And they discovered that helping with hosting Olympic athletes, joining city officials and other local businesses opened doors for future projects and good public relations. Because God rewards Kingdom Business, they are going to get better city connections, more business partnerships, and greater opportunities with future projects, both volunteer and profit making. Also, their city was the host town for international athletes. This business was also making more international connections. Get it?

Consider these questions when considering various community initiatives for your business to take on:

1. Identity: Is the initiative a right match for the nature of the business?
2. Value: How does this initiative add value to the business and vice versa?
3. Operations: Will the initiative fit into the operational flow of the company?
4. People: Can people – employees, vendors, even clients – be involved in the initiative?
5. Growth: Are there positive changes that the initiative will bring to the business?

These questions are not meant so your business can be self-serving when exploring community initiatives. Absolutely not! Rather they will help guide you to the right community initiative, one that fits with the mission of your Kingdom Business. It is essential that you keep true to your vision as a business. One vision.

And please hear this loud and clear – no matter the nature of the project make sure you do the work as a business, not as a charity. Be who God has called you to be. Too often I've seen business try to be like churches and care agencies when what was needed was a really smart business who knew their area of work and could contribute in that way to the initiative. God is not calling you to be anything besides a business. But He is calling you to be a Kingdom Business.

Ready. Set. Build.

There are a great deal of unknowns and changes that may occur, but that's part of the adventure of faith! I tell all the businesses I work with: dream years, plan months, work weeks. Don't simply think about fulfilling projects. Think about building a business. A Kingdom Business. Here's the catch. You already have a plan for your business. You hopefully already have a well-designed strategy. This small book is not meant to change that in anyway. There is no special plan for building a Kingdom Business. Each business is unique in its size, purpose, season and fifty additional variables. There are many great resources available on developing a strategic business plan. I only want to offer a few thoughts to keep in mind as you integrate your Kingdom Calling into your existing business plan.

1. Think sequence.

If you're just starting out, for the first year or two of your work, please make your main goal just to learn. Start small and then scale fast. Be intentional so you can learn from both your mistakes and your failures. One company did not set any "director" in place its first year as the owner truly wanted to learn what the job was like to facilitate the company's community transformation work. After the first phase of learning, he was then ready to hire the right person for this role.

2. Think laboratory.

If you're going to learn and discover all that God wants to show you, you need a laboratory. Experiment. Try different ideas in your business. One construction company took on a project that had to be done in 12 months and required the involvement of its architects, financial planners and facilities management teams. The company was committed to having its people learn so it chose a project that would give them the best opportunity. If you're in this for the long haul, it's wise to use short-term work initially to learn and grow. Then as you gain knowledge and experience your business can launch into more long-term initiatives.

3. Think discovery.

Please, do not try to create a Kingdom Business that is all compartmentalized and wrapped up into a nice neat little micro-managed package right out of the gate. Neither I nor God want Kingdom Called work to be overwhelming or draining for you. Don't think you have to take this on fast and hard. It is so important that you start small, then scale up naturally with skills and lessons gained from each stage or season.

I can't tell you how many businesses have started too fast and taken too many foolish risks, just to shrink back and refuse to build a Kingdom business based on their initial failures. Take a look at the season of your business as part of your planning and realize that you will need to make adjustments as you go. If you didn't, I'd be worried. I've seen too many businesses, owned by Christians, whose business suffers due to the intent of doing "God's mission work." Profits should not always be allocated for mission. Sometimes profits need to be reinvested in the business – which is investing into mission as God is calling you to build a Kingdom Business.

So do not quickly put all profits into a mission project. You need to build your business. Do not quickly alienate your employees, especially your directors. You need them to carry the vision. Do not quickly measure your success before God. Businesses are not built overnight. Neither are Kingdom Businesses. Businesses face many challenges. Kingdom Businesses face those same challenges plus the challenge of a spiritual enemy who wants to destroy your work. Be wise and take your time.

Please never lose sight that you are already operating a Kingdom

Business; you are already doing God's work. Community transformation projects, alongside your profit making projects, are important to the vision and success of a Kingdom Business, but they are to be blessings rather than burdens. They are to enhance your business not drain it.

Benefits of Kingdom Business

There are numerous benefits for a business that has an integrated approach to its Kingdom Calling work. When I say integrated I am referring to a company that has integrated its core objectives, core competencies and its values with a goal towards long-term productivity. I have put them into three categories here, but there is great overlap.

Company Enhancement

The first is company enhancement. Your company just gets better. This happens in so many ways. One that is most obvious is that the identity of the work is attributed to the business and just the individual. It's not all on you the business owner. It's not the great work you've done; it's the great work that your business as an institution did. This drives your reputation, your brand. Your story will generate multiple types of profits.

Integration will also demand that the company's operations and vision are in sync. This eliminates the need for two or three identities that can confuse and compete with each other.

You will learn to create new practices and build new partnerships that will allow you to run your company better and learn from others. One company had to solve a design problem for a community initiative they had taken on. However that problem lead them to design a new software that had application across many of the business's profit-making projects as well. You never know how God might bless your business as you embrace your Kingdom Calling.

Personal Enhancement

That leads me to the second category, personal enhancement. "Now Joel, you just told me it's not all about me." Yep. When I say personal I mean each person, including you. You and your people have the opportunity to have your values challenged and deepened as a result of your Kingdom Business. I mentioned that new untapped fields will be opened up with new opportunities, new friendships, new alignments. This benefits your company, but it also benefits all those that experience healing, growth, and financial prosperity from your company's work. Your employees will feel more valued and invested, like they have purpose to do good for others beyond just their specific job, and this has been shown time and again to produce greater employee retention, loyalty and productivity. It's much easier to hire the right people, especially in the emerging generation, when your business identity is rooted in transforming your world and not just securing profits.

Financial Enhancement

Lastly, but already touched on, financial enhancement. This work cannot *not* translate into growing profits and abundant blessing from God in multiple ways: increased margins and profitability; new untapped markets; new consumers; streamlined practices, awareness of new and better practices, partnerships, employee retention and loyalty, enhanced reputation, and branding in the community associating your company with improving the community. Companies spend a lot of money to gain these things or not lose them in far pricier ways. Furthermore, if you are following Kingdom principles in this work, the Bible is burgeoning with scripture that God will bless you and those involved in a multitude of ways, including financial growth.

Here's a story that illustrates just how God has designed Kingdom Business to impact the world and in return, blesses the business so it has the capacity to have a great impact in the world.

A real estate land development company did some community work (development of low income housing units) in a foreign country that they had never explored as a new market for their business. Through this initiative the company discovered a segment of people in that country wanting to invest in property outside the country. This new market would have never become known had the company not – with pure motivation – shared their expertise with a global community. This new market was a reward from God and a great advancement of the company. God is building His Kingdom businesses and like the ultimate chess player, He places all the pieces in the right positions.

Folks, no gift to God is ever wasted. Quite the opposite in fact. I'm going to call your attention to a section of scripture here from 2 Corinthians 9:7-14 to show you the immeasurable and unforeseen good that comes from work and projects as worship. It is traditionally used in speaking about tithes or offerings, but I want you to look at it with the new eyes that you hopefully have regarding how your work becomes worship. I hope you see how your work and projects become an offering to God when you are operating in your Kingdom Calling with the Creation Mandate as your core vision and aligning with the five Kingdom Business distinctions. Your work and your projects become acts of giving, motivated out of love and gratitude to Him just as meaningful as the money that you tithe through your church. And look what God will do with it.

"Each of you should give whatever you have decided...God loves a cheerful giver." We all recognize this one if we've been in church for any period of time. Ok, so you're giving out of a free heart with your Kingdom Business and your Kingdom projects and God loves it. OK, so you know how God feels about that, but here's what He promises to do with your giving and how it blesses you and glorifies Him. "God will give you His constantly overflowing kindness [grace]. Then, you will always have everything you need, you can do more and more good things." Wow, this is looking really good. But it gets better. "In your lives He will increase the things you do that have His approval." Well we read above that a "cheerful" gift to Him, a gift given motivated by a grateful heart, has His full approval. "God will make you rich enough so that you can always be generous.

Your generosity will produce thanksgiving to God. What you do to serve others not only provides for the needs of God's people, but also produces more and more prayers of thanksgiving to God. You will honor God through this genuine act of service because of your commitment to spread the Good News of Christ and because of your generosity in sharing with them and everyone else. With deep affection they will pray for you because of the extreme kindness that God has shown you." Folks, your giving blesses you with God's grace and abundance. It blesses others so that they will see Him and His incredible love through your work. It will cause them to look to Him and pray for you. God will do more than you could ask or imagine, abundantly. Its His idea of Kingdom Business.

Questions

1. How might you retell your business vision in light of its Kingdom Calling?

2. Which employees could you engage to help lead your business' community projects?

3. How can you keep your motivation pure in building a Kingdom business that honors God?

Chapter Four

Kingdom Business and the Family

"My child, you're always with me.
Everything I have is yours."

Over the years, I've had a majority of the business leaders I work with bring up the issue of family, especially as it relates to transition. I hear, "How do I bring my kids into the company and how do I or *do I* transition myself out?" Transition is an oft-queried area. Along with the topic of business transition, inevitably business leaders also raise the issue of financial transition, namely inheritance. If you have a Kingdom Business, and it's calling is beyond your lifetime and leadership, God wants to bring prosperity so the calling and purpose of the business can continue. This continuance – transitions both in leadership and finances – are critically important issues for a Kingdom Business.

So, the next two sections will address having your kids come in to eventually take over your Kingdom Business and how to transition the wealth, the inheritance both in the present and after you and your spouse have moved into glory. Then at the end of the chapter I will present an idea that I have seen do wonders for family in Kingdom Business. This is the idea of family ministry. Apart from all that you already do in Kingdom Business, how might God use a simple, family ministry initiative, to bless and develop your family culture? We are not just machines for God in business. We are parents who love our children. We are parents who often wonder about the future of our children. We are parents who want to see our children follow in our footsteps of faith in a personal relationship with Jesus. Our Kingdom Calling in business can be a tremendous asset to this, not the detriment it often becomes.

Please recall if you will the opening scene from chapter one of this book. We talked about how important it was to have a vision, one aligned with God and His plan, to drive and guide our lives and work. We talked about how God created the earth and created the Garden of Eden, a prime location with a confluence of rich, lush raw materials that needed developing. Then God assessed His work and judged it to be good, but after a strategic analysis, He determined it could be better if there was a land developer. So, He created "man" to work, to develop and steward those resources.

However, He made one more analysis about this work, it wasn't good to do it alone. Family was created. Man, woman and eventually children to carry on the work. "And God saw that it was good."

God created a family team of husband and wife, a team of slightly different (I know some would say diametrically opposite) beings that each have their talents and gifting to work together in harmony for the purpose of the Creation Mandate that we covered in chapter two. Adam and Eve were to combine their strengths and labor to create and reflect God in doing so and to relish in the abundant life for which God gave them. Ok, sure they blew it, so God gave them children to keep them humble. More coworkers!

The point here is that God, the all-knowing Creator of the universe declared that it wasn't right that work be done alone. Business, work, and your Kingdom Calling were never meant to exclude family. Rather family is to be a combining of talents and human labor. However, there can be a whole host of different combinations of how best to make this situation work well and perhaps just as many ways to have it go poorly since sin is something we must remember to guard ourselves against.

The Bible is rife with lineage and generational transition. Perhaps you now have mind numbing thoughts of the "begats" from Leviticus when I say this, but keep in mind from beginning to end, God clearly values generational transition and family co-laboring. As a Christ follower, you weren't just brought into the family business as a hired hand, but rather you were grafted in through adoption and made an heir to the throne. You'd be hard pressed to find an area that doesn't reflect God's family work design in the Bible, and since we need to "be about the Father's business," we want to model our work lives after the best.

In this chapter, I will discuss three areas: transitioning your kids into your business and transitioning wealth both while you're alive and when you pass on. Finally I'll discuss the idea of family ministry. Because there is a lot of overlap in how to navigate these journeys, I've taken a layered approach like a really good sandwich. What applies to family ministry will also be important to the longevity of your business and the inheritance you lay up for your children and their children.

Transitioning the Kingdom Business to Your Children

Should your kids be involved and eventually takeover the family business? That decision lies in the hands of three people: you, your child and most importantly God. I raise this issue as it has come up in almost every interaction I've had with business owners. Most often the default of the business leader is to take a hands off approach, almost to the point that children would have to initiate any possibility of eventually leading the family business. First and foremost, I'd like to dispel the idea that children should be forced or coerced into running the family business. However a Kingdom Business is not a natural entity. Being created by God, it is divine. It has a divine purpose. There is a Kingdom Calling to you and your business, and thus to your family. Scripture is full of stories where the family – to the unending generation – carried on the initial calling given by God.

Kingdom Business is rarely designed to end with the retirement of its owner. Rarely is Kingdom Business and it's calling solely dependent on one human being, just as a church's sustainability is not dependent on the one pastor. You don't shut down a church when the pastor retires. Nor do you shut down God's business. So, who should carry on, not just the business, but also God's Kingdom Calling? In a family owned business, the children are the prime candidates for this role.

Now you might say, "Joel, I don't want to retire, ever. I get bored not working; I love my work and what I've built with God at the helm." Great! Gonna live forever? Worse, have you witnessed companies that took at least a generation to build a business only to have it destroyed in a blink because no transition was planned, skills weren't learned, children weren't assessed and eased in so they squander the hard work of a life time in less than a decade? I have.

I saw a family in the restaurant business with two sons. The husband and wife were extremely hard working and had the most amazing gift of making you feel like you were a special family guest in their living room, rather than in their bustling and somewhat noisy restaurant. They even had a close, long time friend that acted as an investor and manager. They grew so well that they opened up another restaurant, and then a third. The third was to be a crowning jewel. It was bigger, fancier and hoped to be more profitable than the rest.

By the time the third restaurant was in action, the boys were young adults. They had grown up in and around the restaurant business, or so it seemed. They had learned how to cook and how to greet, but they hadn't been wisely and intentionally groomed in the Kingdom Business. They had their own ideas that the new restaurant should be more like a party nightclub than a family restaurant. They had their own motivation for what they selfishly wanted out of the third restaurant. Now, not to say that change and input aren't good, but these young men weren't basing their entrepreneurial ideas on the core values and identity of the business. They didn't learn how to value people on the staff that had been loyal. They didn't listen to others' ideas. They didn't learn how to make their guests feel like cherished family members when maybe a cook had not made the best meal, or the waitress was slow, or maybe the guests had to wait an hour for a seat (a good problem for a restaurant to have). They wanted to sit up in the office, overseeing the activity with closed-circuit cameras and maybe be present only on the rare occasion. Worse, the parents didn't listen to trusted friends but instead damaged life-long friendships and partnerships when they disregard the counsel of trusted friends who tried to point out that their sons needed better skills training and maturity before allowing them to lead the business.

The family watched two of their restaurants sell at a significant loss, including their crowning jewel. Now they are working incredibly long hours with sore backs and bad knees just to keep a shred of the family business alive. Transition is critical! It's not that the sons could not or should not have taken over the business. It's that the parents had not developed a transition plan from the outset.

The Right Time?

When should you start introducing the family to your business on some level? Yesterday. Research has shown that by age 15, most family patterns have been passed on to the next generation and are lived out thereafter. However, you have no reason to panic if you're starting this later because we serve a God who "makes all things new," so having Him in the equation should help cast out any fears. That being said start as early as you can. Engage your family members into your company vision early and progressively. Bring your kids to work. Let them help out. Give them summer work at the business. Assess formal education, personality, styles and outside work experience as you progressively incorporate your family into your vision and operations.

Now there is a fair amount of debate as to timing and how much detail is to be provided in this process, but in learning from advisors with 30 plus years in the wealth transition field, I recommend a developmental, staged approach. Here you start with the basics and as your child shows interest and capacity, you increase the child's involvement with increasing levels of learning and responsibility as is relevant to age and maturity. Again your goal is not so much to impose, but rather to prepare each family member to the best of his/her capability with communication and active nurturing towards his/her intellectual and spiritual fulfillment. Like all parents, you take a faithful, ongoing role in your children's development. As a business owner, you don't deny that your family has a unique Kingdom Calling with its Kingdom Business. As a parent you want to see what role God may have for your children in your business. What is their Kingdom Calling as it relates to your business identity?

Talk about the Kingdom Business vision with your family. Share the Five Distinctions and integrate progressively. Pray together about the business and pray about how each of you and it can reflect Christ's love. Pray for each other's growth, for patience and for wisdom. You'll need it.

It's About Time

You know, a lot of attention is put on the Prodigal Son story as a beautiful model of God's unfathomable grace for us; as well it should be. But it, along with a whole host of examples are given in the Bible on generations and transitioning of the family business and family income. In this story, we tend to focus on the wilder living, squandering son. The story teaches us about judgment versus grace in how the father rejoices over the return of his wayward son, whereas the eldest son is bitter that his hard work doesn't seem to have been acknowledged. But, there is also an interesting business and wealth transition backdrop in this parable as well. Note, the eldest son, who in that culture and time was guaranteed succession of his father's wealth and due his father's blessing, was working his way up in the business. He comments that he was working in the fields like the slaves, and had done any other task his father had asked of him for years. Now notice his father's response regarding the business and wealth transition, "My child, you're always with me. Everything I have is yours." (Luke 15:31)

This is clearly a parable used by Christ to teach us about grace, but perhaps an additional subtle lesson can be found about children learning the family business and inheritance. This father had his son learn every area of the business and kept him close. He created opportunities to learn for his son and for them to walk through teachable moments together. There is little doubt that the father also knew that the more erratic son needed to go out into the world and learn lessons the hard way before he could come back and have a more humble spirit and strong work ethic. This dad loved his son enough to realize that losing some of the family wealth was worth those immeasurable lessons. Communicate regularly and often. Learn. Spend time and keep close. Again, not the core meaning of this story, but nonetheless an interesting use of a family business parable by Jesus.

I'd like to add one more example here before I go into some more specific nuts and bolts of wealth transition, because it brings a very critical component into the picture. There are so many family examples to choose from in the Bible, ones that went well and ones that went poorly. Jacob (Israel) at the end of his life offers the customary blessings to each of his twelve sons, each completely unique to the boy's style and personality. He even blesses Joseph's two sons, his grandkids, but he does it out of birth order because he listened to God's direction for each of these boys' future. Elijah teaches Elisha in the ways of a prophet through mentorship before he makes his final joyride up to heaven. Job, the man of great suffering, learns to appreciate his blessings, especially his kids, so much so that he bucks cultural tradition of the day and includes his daughters in his will. And Kind David, who so desperately wanted to be the one to build the temple for God, obeyed God's instruction by blessing the son God had chosen for succession. However, David also recognized that Solomon was "young and inexperienced" at the time, so he lined up the plans, the materials, the leadership and the partnerships for his son before announcing him as successor to the kingdom. He also gave him great advice to listen to God, seek God, and obey God as a general rule for success in any endeavor, but especially as a leader. All these stories show leaders that spent time teaching, observing, imparting, praying, listening and were intentional with the task of progressive wealth or business transition.

Give Time

But there's one more component that runs as a common thread in each of these succession stories to which I'd like to call attention, the relationship of God the Father to His Son Jesus. Scripture tells that Jesus, in addition to learning a trade (probably his earthly father Joseph's business), was also learning His Heavenly Father's business all along the way. In fact, His earthly parents misplaced Him for three days as a young boy because He was "in His father's house" learning.

There's much preparation and prayer that went into Jesus before He officially began His ministry, no doubt. But there was one defining moment between the Father and the Son for all to see. Jesus goes about the requirements of the religious culture of that time. He has John the Baptist baptize Him. Jesus knows it's important to be in order. And as He comes out of the water, what happens? God audibly announces for all present to hear, "This is my Son, whom I love; with Him I am well pleased." He has trained His son, His son has learned, His son is ready and now God, the Father blesses His Son publically to announce the succession. The witnesses, and thanks to the Bible writers, we all witness that God approved of His son and felt He was now equipped to take on His destiny in the family business.

Do your children know you approve of them joining you in business? Have they spent time with you learning what you do, why God called you to this, where do you believe God has called your Kingdom Business? Have you heard what they think is God's calling for them? And do those in your business: your leadership, your partners, your clients know that you have nurtured this transition and are ready to oversee or even remove yourself as your heir steps in to make his or her way and make you proud? Perhaps they should. A public passing of the mantle and endorsement go a long way in the business world.

Transitioning God's Wealth To Your Kids: Inheritance

I'll tell you honestly that there are people with a lot more knowledge, a lot more credentials and a lot more skill than myself that get paid a lot more money for their part in helping business leaders with all the necessary rules, laws, documents, and paths to fiscally safe and sound wealth transition. So, I'll cover this topic from a different perspective.

1. Be intentional.

This is one area of life that you do not want to "wing it". Make an intentional effort to learn what wealth vehicles you need to have money transitioned to your family now and later. Do you need a will and/or a trust? Probably. Is the business in a separate trust feeding the family trust? Learn what you can about legal structures, asset allocation, and asset protection. Realize that you will need trusted and well-vetted advisors for these areas. Don't leave it for "someday" later. Plan early and review regularly. But also realize, that while you should make efforts to be educated, wealth transition probably isn't your Kingdom Calling; it is someone else's that is there to help.

Peter Riley, a learned wealth transition advisor of 30 plus years says, "What each family needs is one or more individuals who are across the entirety of the family activities and can reconcile the flow-on implications and risks associated with the advice received on any specific matter." Know that these trusted advisors are likely to ebb and flow, as your children become adults with their own trusted individuals with whom they prefer to work. A family trustee or advisor is a critical role to be agreed upon and vetted.

Make sure any advisors and additions to the family (spouses, etc.) know the family philosophy, the culture, your mission statement, and your family's core values. Also, consider things like, should wealth go into the hands of a family member that is in the role or profession that exposes him/her to litigation? Probably not, but shelters can be set up to handle this. Also, are there members that clearly aren't ready to handle or manage wealth themselves? This is obviously part of the decision making process than can and should be planned for.

Its important is to be intentional, document the family philosophy, consciously nurture relationships, learn yourself, your family, and your advisors, and keep God as your key tour guide on this wild adventure.

2. Be visionary.

But also realize that as Peter Smiley says, "If you are not growing the family wealth, it will slowly decline, so each generation must be wealth creators." Your Kingdom Business needs following generations for it to flourish. It is not enough to simply handover wealth to your children. They need to know how to generate more wealth with the inheritance you give them. You need to have a long-term vision for your business that far outlives you. Your children can only sustain and increase the business if their inheritance is seen as a seed for the future and not as the finished fruit to enjoy today.

3. Be multi-generational.

Often the Bible refers to the "third" generation when speaking of inheritance. God isn't just interested in the next generation. He's interested in the *every* next generation. He instructs us to be aware of our great-grandchildren and onwards.

Remember, God is the God of generations, all working together. A generational business is not just a business that your children takeover when you are out of the picture. A Kingdom Business is one where the generations engage with each other in specific roles. Consider the special bond of grandparent to grandchild. Taking the example of Abraham, Isaac and Jacob as a pattern for your generational roles, consider that Abraham's role was to create the industry for Isaac. Isaac's role was to bless Jacob to continue by giving him authority. Jacob, then as the youngest in the generation, carried a great respect for Abraham and the family heritage.

To build a family business there must be continued investment and expansion, an ongoing release of authority and a rich honor for the family's heritage. All the generations must build this together and this doesn't usually happen by accident, but with care and intention.

The way God intends His family to function is for us to learn from the previous generations, taking everything they have acquired and passed on, incorporating that into the things God teaches us personally. Thus mingling the gifts, knowledge, and strengths of each. Then, we pass on all of that to every next generation.

It is wrong for a new generation to have to start over. There should never be an older generation saying, "We had to learn the hard way, so figure it out on your own," or a younger generation saying, "We don't need what you experienced and learned, we have something new."

Its right for the upcoming generation to build on the struggles you have overcome. That's what is most effective for the business. What's not right is if they don't identify and confront their own challenges of faith in the business. You jumped off a cliff in faith when you launched your family business. You built a solid business foundation. Allow your children to build further by not holding back that solid foundation from them. But also inspire them to identify their own faith cliff that will take the business to the next level. Each generation will certainly have its unique challenges and God may do some things for and with them that were unknown to the previous generation. But to achieve what I believe God is calling your Kingdom Business to become and to have the maximum impact upon the world for God's Kingdom, you must include and build together generationally.

There is no silver bullet to achieving effective family wealth transition. It will take focus, discipline and process. But remember, your ever present Father is happy to impart wisdom and assistance in this or any other adventure He's called you to. Enjoy the ride. Wear a seatbelt. Put your hands in the air...towards Him.

Family Ministry: Creating a legacy beyond business

Families have habits and various characteristics that identify them as a family. They celebrate Christmas in a certain way. They have their own language that only family members know. They are defined, not just by a collection of individuals but also by being one together as a family. Many families don't have family ministry as a shared identity. Often the individual members have their own ministry in which they serve. This service is important and provides meaning to their individual lives. Other family members celebrate these various individual expressions of ministry. But family ministry is not a collection of individual ministry that families celebrate. Family ministry is when a family, together, determines how it can, together, make a difference for God's

Kingdom. Individuals have ministry. Churches have ministry. We are discovering that even your business has ministry. Why not have your family have ministry? But not as a business, or a church, or an individual, but rather as a family. This is an extra "icing" that God gives us as a family. Now when we sit around at Christmas, sharing our lives. We also collaborate on those family initiatives that makeup our family ministry.

Why is this idea so crucial to Kingdom Business? Tragically, many families suffer when owning and operating a business. Parents spend long hours away from the children. Church takes a back seat to the business needs. Money can be plentiful, but then leads family members down a dangerous road, away from life-giving faith in Christ.

Family ministry is not the save-all answer to this dilemma. But it does help a great deal as it refocuses the family together, to what really matters in life. Family ministry keeps the family keenly aware of the Lordship of Christ and the identity of its Kingdom Business. It gives a unique and wonderful story to tell as part of the family heritage. People want their lives to count. Sometimes business, even Kingdom Business, doesn't answer that need. Family ministry does.

Not too dissimilar to the involvement of leadership, management, employees, clients and partners, I want to offer a somewhat systematic approach to how we involve family in our work. But before we go into family vision, mission, assigning leadership roles, etc, I'd like to make a strong advisement. Get to know your family, not individually but as a single name, a lineage and a heritage. Discover how God has used your family in the past and what grace seems to be on your family for the present.

Not that *you* ever would, but it's important to guard against a Godfather type approach to family ministry, forcing a round peg into a square hole without acknowledgement for God's unique plan for the family. As a business creator and/or owner, there is a high likelihood that you are a highly driven, hard working risk taker type. Whatever life events, good or bad got you to this place; they shaped you to be the leader you are today. In order to bring others into this party, you need to first be willing to not go it alone as a maverick type but also, you must know what makes your family tick and how your family members can serve together.

A family leader must be aware of him or herself in order to know where to guide, nurture, to be patient, to teach or to listen, otherwise your efforts can be misguided, misinterpreted, or become dysfunctional and harmful and "a house divided cannot stand" so we don't want that.

Family ministry provides purpose and spiritual growth that God has designed for each and all of you in symphony, and so it is to be approached with care, respect and seen as an opportunity rather than a necessity just for keeping the financial capital intact or multiplying. Family ministry is an opportunity to actively nurture each member towards his or her personal physical, emotional, and spiritual fulfillment and contentment.

Family DNA

Just like your business, your family needs a sense of its Kingdom Calling and vision. You know the vision for your company, but determine together with your spouse and your children, what will be the family ministry focus. What are your family's values? Values will be a fundamental cornerstone on which to guide development and function as a checklist when looking at choices, decisions or challenges for family ministry. Of course your values should be biblically based, but your family will have its own culture as it were. And that will more than likely shift as your children grow into adulthood to bring their own experiences and hopefully maturity into the mix. As they age, welcome your kids into the adjustment and setting of the family values that will serve to create your family mission statement. Also, though you may operate within your values privately, you will need to ultimately share these with key third parties such as new spouses, independent directors, and/or key advisors.

I know a family whose heritage is in great missionary work. Grandparents, at great risk and immeasurable faith, lived their entire lives in another cultural context. The adult children have all adopted children from global regions. For this family, children-at-risk and the global village are critical factors in its values, identity and ultimately, ministry expression as a family.

Your family values will comprise your sense of family mission. Some families even choose to draft a family constitution all distilled as a governing, but amendable family document. This governance system will help define your family ministry focus. It's okay if you're not this deliberate and by-the-book, but please make it a priority one way or the other to know your family's core values and determine how they will shape your family ministry.

For example, will your family ministry be framed by a certain location in the world? A certain type of work? A certain type of person or need that exists in a community? Many families find it helpful to compile a short list of criteria that determine what their family ministry will look like? Take the time to talk as a family to see where each of you feels led and how you can all work as a team to create, reflect and bless. Do this periodically, because age, environment, and revelation can necessitate edits.

Take it one STEP at a time

I've created what I call the STEP Planning Guide for developing your family ministry. It's a simple step-by-step process for families that are just starting out with the idea of creating a family ministry.

S - Start with the right person.

The right person is both defined by roles within the family and the people and partners the family comes alongside in its ministry. People always trump projects. This comes by observing strengths, weaknesses, and personalities and matching them up with the project at hand. And this is not just looking for a leader per se, this is for all the roles. Does one member of your family exhibit better organizational skills than another? This individual might be best as a coordinator processing financial requests, project oversight, communications and support. Is there another person that is more skilled at leadership? Make this person that point person for project development, caring for partners and other family members and prayer for the team. Another key role is an executive role. This person should be good with oversight of finances, vision development and executive issues. Is there a family member with a passion for prayer? Let the person's passion define that individual's participation. Note that these roles may change with a different project and as physical and spiritual maturity take place, new placement may make itself more evident. Remain open to this flow.

T – Take on one small, one-off project.

Remember as we discussed in chapter three, as you begin, your goal is simply learning. What role does God have for each of you and your family as a team? Perfectionists often procrastinate because they can never get started. Dive in but take it small to start. At the start, find a project your family can fulfill but without a long-term commitment. This way you can accomplish something, learn together but not be locked into a ministry commitment for an unforeseeable future. This first project should not be any longer than 6-8 months in length and should only have a small financial commitment to it. Your goal is not just to write a check as a family. It's to engage the family members through commitment, prayer, engagement with hurting people, and a gifting and passion-based expression of God's love to others.

E – Evaluate the family work.

What did you learn about the project, the people, and any partnerships that may have been created? Did your quiet kid shock you and step out fearlessly to handle an unforeseen problem? Ah, leadership restructuring for the next go around. Did you take on a water well project and learn that a member of your family loathes being near the water but is energized by working in the very nearby mountains that you had to go to get supplies? Learn. Pay attention. Grow. Adjust. Most importantly, ask the question, "What did God show us about Himself in our family?" As much as ministry is about others, it's also important to discern how God will use this family ministry to grow and spiritually mature your family. As a family, reflect on both the work and how it affected each family member. Maybe some didn't feel very involved at all? And discover how they thought it affected the family as a whole?

P – Position your family.

As your family begins to engage in family ministry projects, you'll see them fit into one of three categories, as part of your learning and planning for the future. Some projects, when they are completed, will be done for good. This is work, both the project and the family roles, that were beneficial as much was learned, but you realize for a variety of reasons that it is not a project type not to be repeated.

Some projects, when completed, will be considered to be a one-off kind of work. This is a project, good for one-off type projects but not for the long-term ministry of the family. Additional projects, like serving together at a Thanksgiving Day feeding program could be done, and would be both right and fulfilling, but they won't be core to the family ministry.

Finally, you will do projects, especially at the outset, where the work just feels right. The project is based on a partnership that the family cherishes and is ready to advance to the next stage of work. Family members see how they can participate and sense a measure of ownership with the ministry. This work defines the family ministry profile. So, this type of family ministry work naturally leads to how the family will build for the future.

Remember, none of this is accomplished overnight. Enjoy the process. Celebrate each good work the family does, even if it is not to be repeated. Take your time so that in a few years, the work you are doing, is genuinely true to your family identity and God's Kingdom Calling on your family. Keep in the forefront of your mind, that this Kingdom work will hopefully bless others but it can also bring great blessing to you and your family if in just the spiritual growth that is facilitated. Keep the family ministry relational (people matter) and spiritual (keep God as the CSO). Simply continue to build, one season at a time, sharing the work and the joy of serving together as a family.

Family matters. Family is God's plan of evangelism. It is His plan for fulfilling both the Great Commission and the Creation Mandate. Family however is never easy, especially family business. Rather than avoid family with business, attempting to compartmentalize each far away from the other, seriously consider integrating both. Of course family matters cannot solely be defined by business. Kids have sports games parents should attend. Family vacations should be fun and not work. Moms and dads should have romantic getaways, completely unrelated to business, that make them far better parents.

But leverage the gift of Kingdom Business to embrace your Kingdom Calling as a family calling. You have been given a unique opportunity to build a family, based on God's love and His Word,

Joel Holm

with His calling in business. What you do now matters for generations to come.

Questions

1. What can you do to engage your children more into the Kingdom Called family business?

2. Who can you look to for assistance in setting up the proper legal structures for inheritance in your family?

3. What first steps could you take to try out the family ministry idea?

Chapter Five

Kingdom Business and Your Local Church

"I am the vine. You are the branches.
All who live in me as I live in them will produce much fruit."

I asked you in the beginning of this book to catch a vision, a vision of your life as a part of a bigger story that God is writing with you. I hoped that you would fully grasp this idea that you are part of a grand scheme not just as a person, but also as a business leader and even a business owner. You and your work, your business, are a part of God's vast Kingdom. In this book we've discussed various aspects about what it means to be Kingdom Called and to harness the power of business to change the world. In this final chapter, it's important that you truly see where you fit in the grand scheme of God's Kingdom. So you can see how you and your business matter. So you can see the profound, wide reaching effect you can have for God and His Kingdom when you nestle comfortably into His design.

The Kingdom

First, let's take a look at what exactly is God's Kingdom. Not so easy to define. In fact, in the Bible, God's Kingdom is referred to in a myriad of ways. It's called a remnant, a precious possession, a royal priesthood and a wedding feast that all are welcome to crash. It's likened to a mustard seed, yeast, wheat hidden among the weeds, a barren fig tree, and a hidden treasure and a pearl, both worth giving everything for. Now, I can't really say why God, the Bible writers and Jesus chose to give so many metaphors to describe God's great Kingdom, but it causes me to think that there is a purpose for it. Maybe God doesn't want His Kingdom to be easily pigeonholed.

We use the word Kingdom a bit in our lives but far more we use the word church. How does the Bible define the church? The Bible gives a multitude of metaphors for the Kingdom and then also makes a point to give as many metaphors about the church, with varying and necessary parts. So, for the rest of this chapter in the interest of simplicity, I'd like to create two labels. I'd like to identify the Kingdom as the Church with a capital C. It's the One Church of which all churches, ministries, disciples and celestial beings are all par of. The second label is that of the local church. You know, the one you go to each weekend that you belong to as a member. That I'll label as the church with the little c. Note, the little c is most definitely not an indicator of importance of one over the other. Your church is a critical piece of God's Kingdom (Church), actually even leading the way with Christ at the head. So let's use these two labels, Kingdom and local church.

See, I think God is pointing out that the Kingdom and your local church are designed and operate best with variety, but as diverse parts that work in concert. There should never be a one size fits all other than Jesus. Each individual and every church has its own flavor and style. Of course, God has to be the central force within this, but uniqueness is part of God's plan. Every local church follows God's Word so at the core of it, we are all the same. However how we express God's design is where our uniqueness comes in. Think of it. Jesus didn't have to make each person with a unique set of fingerprints, but He did. Why? Why not give every believer *all* the gifts of the Holy Spirit all in one? We'd be awesome, like Christian super heroes! But, then we wouldn't need each other. And we wouldn't be needed by each other. The Bible says we are known by the fruit of the Spirit as we produce or do good works in expression of love to Him.

You see there is such a powerful witness for God when all the various parts work together in harmony that it shows, often even without words, that God is real, that His Kingdom is real and that Christ is the head of the body. When people of all walks, businesses, ministries, missionaries, churches and more all join in Kingdom work, it sends a powerful message to a world of watching eyes for God. When all the wildly different parts fit where they belong and operate in unity for God - mountains move and God gets the glory.

We do this uniquely, creatively but also in unity with each other. We do this as members in a local church and we do this as members in His Kingdom. As a Kingdom Business leader you have a specific role in each.

So how does your Kingdom Business, your own personal life and your local church all fit together into God's Kingdom Calling for you?

Your Kingdom Business, operating in its unique identity, fits as part of a big beautiful mosaic called the Kingdom. Kingdom Business is not local church. Your local church, just like your business, is also part of God's Kingdom. God's Kingdom includes not just your business and your local church however. It includes non-profits, NGOs, ministries, families, hospitals, schools, and more are all a part of the Kingdom. Now you're beginning to see why God uses so many diverse metaphors for His Kingdom in Scripture. So, for simplicity's sake, I want you to take the macro view that your company, operating in its Kingdom Calling is part of the Kingdom of God, transforming this world.

Then, paramount to your life, is your role in your own local church. You, as an individual, have a vitally important role to play as a member of your local church. So you as a business owner, play a part in God's Kingdom and you as a Christ-follower, play a part of God's local church. Why does this matter? It's important to understand the distinction as it affects the role you play in both.

I want you to understand clearly, that *each* is necessary. Your business belongs to the Kingdom and you belong to the local church. One does not alleviate the need for the other and one is not any more important than the other. Both are part of God's plan where variety truly is the spice of life. So let's look at what it means to be a member in your church and what it means for your company to be a member in God's Kingdom.

Your role in God's local church

Let's now look at your individual membership to the church. This is your local fellowship where you gather weekly or more to feed your soul, learn about God and Christ through sermons and your Bible, and join in unity with other beautifully imperfect believers to nourish both your church and the community that it serves. Again, your church, is a unique member of the Kingdom, having its own size, style, flavor, and expression of Christ.

I want you to see that you as a person fit in your church, as a member. This is where you participate, grow, tithe and support the leadership of your church. All these actions are of supreme importance to your faith and to the Great Commission. Your place in your local church is an important part of God's plan for your local church. It's important to see this role almost apart from your business role. Otherwise the temptation would be to see your local church only through the filter of your business's calling.

Participate

In your church, my hope is that you'll carryout four important roles: participate, tithe, grow and support. By participate I mean, that you would attend services regularly, that you would build relationships with fellow believers, and that you would find a place to serve within your church. Perhaps this is the place where you don't have to be and don't want to be in charge of anything. Perhaps here is where you are a greeter, or an usher or you sing on the worship team. Or conversely, maybe you want to use your leadership skills to lead ministry outreaches to convalescent homes or jails. The point here is that you are an active, involved member of your church. Don't overcomplicate it. Participate.

To use an example from an earlier chapter, if you make really great signs as your Kingdom Calling, then maybe your business will make signs for a banquet for homeless people. But maybe you, as the business owner, also serve as a musician in your church. Different flavors. Each needed. Each vital. Stay rooted in your church or it is likely the rest will never even come to fruition. Jesus said we can produce much fruit when we stay connected to the vine and nothing without. Fruit comes in all sorts of shapes, colors, sizes and flavors too.

Tithe

This leads to tithing. Your church nurtures you and the surrounding community it serves. This is one of those flavors of how God can be seen showing His love through others. And though God is the ultimate source and doesn't need your money back, He knows that it feeds your soul to give 10% of your income in faith and obedience to Him, and that the church can then use that resource to spread the Good News and God's love to others. It's wonderful to say, "God bless you" and pray for someone who can't afford heat in the home, but it's also critically tangible to bless them with blankets, food or maybe help with the bills. It's all an expression of God's love.

But what I want to drive home here and throughout this chapter is that the tithe to your church, is your offering from you as an individual. Often I am asked about the distinction between the income earned personally and the profits gained from a business. I believe the Bible teaches that your personal income is tithed to the local church whereas God gives you great latitude in what you do with the business profits. You should not exempt yourself from tithing to your church because of the Kingdom work your business does nor should you feel required to only give money from your business to your local church. Both are very important and both are necessary, but different.

Grow

I mentioned that tithing is part of spiritual growth. Grow is the third thing that I hope you'll do as a member of your church. God has promised in His word that He will continue and complete the work in you that He began when you became a believer, so have faith that He is going to continue to form you more and more in the likeness of His son, Jesus. Why not cooperate. He does this primary through your participation in the local church. He doesn't want you to replace the role of the local church for spiritual growth with your ministry work in your business.

Just as a pastor should not replace his ministry role in a church for his own personal devotion to Christ, so to the business leader should not rely on his Kingdom business for his identity with Christ. He wants you to know Him deeper, to become stronger in faith, have confident trust in Him, and to enjoin others in this wonderful journey.

Remember, each of the parts of the body need to work together. Get to know the nose that sits down the row from you and the arm in front of you and even the mouth down front. You need each other. You are a community of believers that can support each other, learn from each other, love each other and grow in Christ's love. Your pastor leads you, but you guys are in this together. Do community together in your church.

Support

That brings up another important member - your pastor. Sure your pastor is the leader of this individual flock. He has been imbued with authority in spiritual matters in the church, but not over every aspect of your life. He may be gifted at speaking and interpreting the Bible for you. He or she will guide you in spiritual growth. This is simply where God has called your pastor. But, in case you were ever wondering, every pastor is human. They have struggles and flaws just like you and everyone else. Every local church pastor has an enormously challenging and at times incredibly difficult job. There is great weight with great responsibility. His job is to feed you spiritually, but he may have times when he's revved up and raring to go, and he may also have times when his faith is being tried just like yours. Sometimes, especially when interacting with affluent business leaders, a pastor can become a bit insecure.

The thing here to realize, and perhaps you as a business leader can identify quite well with, is that he is a leader, a public figure and a voice for God in this case, but he is also a person. He needs your support, your encouragement and your prayers. He is part of this big diverse body just like you as a member of your church. His "business" is a part of the Kingdom, as is yours. Don't let your role in your Kingdom Business too greatly define your relationship with your pastor. This is the critical error I've seen happen numerous times, creating an awkward relationship between a pastor and a business leader. He or she needs you as a friend far more than anything else.

When you define your role with the pastor by your business, money always plays the major part in this. In worst-case scenarios, the business leader uses his or her wealth to gain access to the pastor. Or the pastor leverages his authority to gain access to the business leaders' wealth. But these are worst-case scenarios. Most often, the relationship is not so manipulative. It's just awkward. I believe it is the responsibility of the business leader to lead the relationship and set the tone of the relationship with the pastor. I also believe it is the role of the pastor but since this book is not about them, let's talk about your leadership role.

A friend owned a business that provided home interior design. The city asked the business for help in designing public housing space. The business – being a Kingdom Business – saw this as a golden opportunity to live out its calling, core to its values and skills. Then my friend got an idea. He contacted the pastor and proposed that the church engage its members to volunteer in this public housing project by setting up the designs the business had put in place for the city. The church was partnering with the business but the business was leading it. The business was offering a great opportunity to the church (with little administrative effort and not cost to the church) to be involved in community transformation.

Three results came about by this. First, the pastor discovered again that the business leader truly had the best interests of the church in mind. This business provided a great win for the church in its mission work. Second, the business owner linked his business to the church, without having to be controlled by the church. The idea was generated by the business. The expense was covered by the business. The business was not just a subset of the local church. And finally, the pastor and the business owner built trust together. Leading is serving. This business leader served his pastor and his church. And in doing so, continued the development of a healthy relationship with his pastor.

A Kingdom Business will partner with many members in God's Kingdom. But when possible, be intentional so your Kingdom Business can develop a healthy, mutually beneficial relationship with your local church.

Your Business' Role in God's Kingdom

I confess I have an agenda. I have had one from the very beginning of this book. It's fruit. Lots and lots of it. Fruitfulness for God and His Kingdom. That's fruit that lasts forever.

I very much want this little book to give you a vision for your work life that can truly make a measurable and profound difference in this world for God in a way that only comes through the business. So many people live their lives and wonder what really mattered in all the hours they spent on this planet, "Did I make a difference; what was it all about?" You don't need to ever say that. You are uniquely poised to literally change the world. As the leader and owner of a Kingdom Business, you are part of His Kingdom. You can either be a non-participating member who never shows up to any meetings and wonders if you still are part of the membership or you can do a whole lot of good for God as a contributing member of His Kingdom. Here's how: serve, partner, and influence.

Serve

A company president learned through his membership in his local service club about a nonprofit organization that serves foster children who have been split from their siblings. This company president realized he had the skill, the resources and the heart to serve through his business. He partnered with the nonprofit organization to host a career day for these foster kids to give them exposure to work skills that they might not otherwise receive. He used his background, position, company and ability to serve these at-risk kids.

When his pastor discovered that the company, owned by one of his members, had done this work the business owner got nervous. At first he thought the pastor would be upset, wondering why he wouldn't use the business to help the local church first. The owner was gratefully surprised one day when he received a phone call from the pastor, commending him for the service his business had done for God's Kingdom in partnership with the nonprofit organization. He realized that his pastor had a Kingdom vision and heart. He also realized that his faithfulness in serving in his local church had built a trust and credibility that made it easy for the pastor to celebrate the business owners' ministry outside the local church.

My point, which I'm betting you're getting by now, is that as a leader, as a business owner, you are gifted with certain views and skills that make you the perfect person to help serve in the big beautiful Body of Christ, the Kingdom, with your Kingdom Business.

It's been said in so many ways that the greatest leaders serve. Forbes has a list of the best leadership quotations filled with people who understood and lived this age-old principle. Jesus most certainly did. People came from all around in droves to listen to Christ, to hear His message of hope. He led a team of disciples that gave up lives and livelihood to follow the leader. He inspired this and so much more by serving. "Your leader must be like a servant...But I'm among you as a servant." (Luke 22:19)

Use your leadership gifting, not just in your business but also through your business in the world. As a leader, you are perfectly equipped to serve, and by serving, your work can become worship, and your business will be a powerful partner in the Kingdom.

Partner

That leads right into your second task. Partner. Remember I said you don't have to do this alone and you aren't meant to. Actually it's almost impossible to do God's Kingdom work alone. He made it that way. He's as interested in how we serve together as He is in what we accomplish for Him. Ever heard the quotation that goes something like this? "If you think you're too small to make a difference? Try spending the night with a mosquito." What about a locust? One bug. Not much. But a horde of them can be a biblical plague. Similarly a horde of Kingdom Businesses can be a biblical-sized epic blessing for this world.

I'm not saying you're a bug, but I am saying that partnerships can multiply the difference you make. I want to share an example here of partnership in the Kingdom that is changing the world.

Dr. Kent Bradley was a medical missionary in Liberia. However, in the recent Ebola breakout, he contracted the disease. Despite taking what seemed every precaution to avoid contracting the disease, he became one of those he was there to serve.

Unbeknownst to Kent, somewhere else in the world, there is a business owner that makes mp3 players. Not the major bells and whistles mp3 player but one that can be preloaded with audio material and played over and over. It is essentially designed to be disposable to keep costs down. This business owner has partnered with a ministry in its initiative to get the Good News to people in as many languages as a possible and as simply as possible to every part of the world for as little cost as possible. This business owner is operating in his Kingdom Calling to make disposable mp3 players that play audio files long enough to introduce people to Christ. But let's get back to Dr. Bradley.

As part of his fight for his life, he had to go into isolation in order to not infect others. No family, no friends, not much in the way of amenities in his developing world surroundings, but plenty of time to rest, pray and listen to sermons on a simple mp3 player that was preloaded with the Word of God, over and over again. It is said, "faith comes by hearing the Word." Dr. Bradley was closed off from the world but thanks in part to a business owner operating in his Kingdom Calling he wasn't cut off from God's precious, life-giving Word. He beat the odds. He survived Ebola!

Now I do want to take a moment here to address an item of partnerships - who. Here, in this prior example, this business owner partnered with an international ministry. I can't recommend strongly enough that businesses partner with other ministries, local churches, NGOs, missionaries and other businesses. Everyone would agree.

But what about non-faith based organizations or non-believers? There is tremendous potential for displaying the power of God in these relationships when they are developed. I would simply caution that you be *very* wise with whom you choose to partner. I'm not saying don't partner with non-believers. Quite the opposite. I'm saying realize there might be a different set of rules this company or individual is operating under and that you need to stick close to God in these ventures. The Bible says, "Worldly people are more clever than spiritually-minded people when it comes to dealing with others." And to "Be as wary as snakes and harmless as doves."

Remember that you may be the only exposure these people have had to Christ and that you will need to invite God into this situation even if it's only silently. Stay in close touch with God through prayer and listen very well for He promises to guard you and guide you. You may be the perfect water to a seed that someone else planted in this person or you may be planting the seed for the first time. "Be gentle and respectful" as 1 Peter teaches.

Influence

This leads directly to the third task. You and your business can help change the world by joining a movement of business owners operating in their Kingdom Callings with their Kingdom Businesses making His Kingdom come. I'm passionate about this because as I've worked with business owners and leaders around the world for the past years, I've seen both a need and a power when Christian business leaders gather together, leaning on each other, influencing each other to fulfill their Kingdom Calling.

All over the world I've discovered business leaders facing the same fears, questions, dreams and prayers that you are. They want to make a difference. They are not sure what to believe. Many having been told that their business is either a necessary evil or simply exists to fund the church. But the Spirit of God is at work in them. They know there is more to this. But alone, few will take the necessary steps to "harness the power of business to change the world." They need friends, on the same journey, who they can trust.

This is why God has given you the leadership gift of influence. Influence is not the same thing as expertise. None of us are fully clued in to what God is doing. But we are moving forward. Don't move forward alone. Be an influence on other business owners, on workers, on clients and vendors, all trying to figure out how their faith should intersect with their business world.

You don't need to have all the answers. You do need to see that God has positioned you to influence others to seek out His Kingdom Calling, alongside of you.

I want you to see that your work matters. I want you to see increased profits of the personal and financial kind. I want you to see how your business can make a difference, alongside thousands of others. Together Kingdom Businesses change the face of a community. They rally the masses to bring God's values and hopes to a community.

Hurting people are convinced that God can't possibly be real or care about them, but they will now see as God uses the knowledge, skill and yes, the heart of a business to show His amazing love to them in a very real way. You can do this when you fully grasp the vision of the Creation Mandate. You were made to work this amazing creation of earth for the benefit of yourself and all of God's creation. You were meant to profit from that and use those profits to bless others in your family, in your business, in your clientele, and around the world. You were meant to reflect God in your work and your actions. You were meant to fill up with gratitude for the abundant blessing that your business has seen when it aligns with the Five Distinctions of a Kingdom Business so much that you want to branch out into projects that bless others more and make God smile at how well you've managed the profits He's given you.

Trust me, God will give you that opportunity. "Whoever can be trusted with very little can also be trusted with a lot." (Luke 16:10) You can then inspire other business owners to want to join you in your projects or simply learn why you're so blessed and ask how you do it. I need you to really "get" the principles in this book so you can walk this out and encourage other business leaders to do the same. Then you can see what it looks like when it's one of many joining forces.

You know, it certainly isn't by accident that the story of the rich man and his business manager is part of the Bible. Some people get caught up in the isolated statement, "you can't serve God and mammon (money)." Sure it's true. Money can never be your goal! Dishonest use of money will never produce good fruit. We've all heard the slightly misquoted verse, "money is the root of all evil." One little tiny word makes a big difference. The verse is actually "money is *a* root of all evil."

You see, tremendous good can be done with financial profits. Jesus said to use your wealth to make friends, to give to those in need, and to tithe. Furthermore, Deuteronomy 8:18 says, "Always remember that it is the Lord your God who gives you power to become rich." And Proverbs 10:22 says, "The blessing of the Lord makes a person rich, and He adds no sorrow with it." God wants His people to live in blessing and abundance and to be good stewards of that blessing.

We know that wealth distribution is a godly trait. But wealth distribution takes wealth creation. However being Kingdom Called is far more than making money to give it away. It's realizing how and why God included work into our divinely created identity and how He now uses the marketplace for His Kingdom purpose.

You are meant to work. You were wired for it. You were meant to make the most of what God has provided to live in His abundant blessing and to bless others. You were never made to do this alone. God designed family to be a part of this, and for partnerships to happen so as to make this abundant life available to everyone throughout this hurting creation of God's. As a business leader, you are the perfect person with the right gifting, the tools, and hopefully after reading this book, a little more knowledge to join others and be a difference maker.

I told you I had an agenda from the beginning of this book. I want you to catch a vision. I want to inspire you and have you help make this message spread like wildfire, a fire for hope for those that are in cold darkness. The Law of Diffusion of Innovation says that you cannot achieve mass market penetration until you get between 15 - 18% of the population on board. Then, it takes off. I only need 15-18% of business owners to catch this vision, operate in it and then it can take off. Help me change the world. Help me bring hope. Be one of the 15-18% and bring others into this emboldened minority that will then attract the majority. You are equipped. You have the best business partner you could ever imagine if you just invite Him to be the CEO.

How do you do this? Reach out to other business leaders and simply share your journey together. Learn from each other. Pray together. Be members of God's Kingdom together.

There was another metaphor for God's Kingdom that I didn't include in the beginning that I'd like to leave you with. It's the story of the three servants. It starts like this, "The kingdom of heaven is like a man going on a trip." Hey, it starts with a businessman going on vacation. Already you say, "I'm in!" Ok, it says he's going on a trip, but I like to think it's a vacation. He calls three servants and entrusts various sums of money to them, it says based on their abilities. The first two invest their respective sums and double the investment. 100% ROI. That'll do right? The third servant, who received the least portion of funds (based on his ability), buries his portion for safekeeping.

The businessman is furious when he returns. He says, "You could've at least put it in the bank and earned interest!" So, he takes the small portion and gives it to the most enabled servant who doubled his largest portion.

I know this parable isn't really about money exclusively. It's about the Kingdom. You are an able and equipped servant. Go make the most of what has been entrusted to you. Take the other servant that also knew how to double his investment with you. Use the skills, knowledge and gifting that God has helped you develop. Without vision, people perish. I hope I've given you a vision of a happy ending to a story that God would be happy to be told over and over again.

Membership in God's Kingdom and membership in God's local church can be seen in so many ways. It's a gift. It's a right. It's a calling. It's a responsibility. It's a relationship. However you determine to label it, never forget that God never separates your faith, your work and your membership in His Body. He sees them as intricately intertwined with each other. When you see that as well, then they all flourish. If any one of them takes too strong a role over the others, then they are all negatively affected.

Maybe the best label for membership in God's Kingdom and God's local church is mystery. None of us quite know exactly how the whole thing works. But we trust the one Head of His Church and the Head of His Body, our Lord Jesus Christ.

We rely on Christ for the leadership role in our faith, our work, our family and our church. As much as we are called business leaders, the truth is we have never been more of a follower in our lives then when we embrace fully our membership in God's Kingdom and church.

Questions

1. What new possibilities come to mind when you view your business and your local church as co-laborers in the God's Kingdom?

2. Do you need to strengthen your role in your local church?

3. How can you influence other business owners in the idea of Kingdom Called: Harnessing the Power of Business to Change the World?

Conclusion

A conservative estimate of how your adult life is spent is that you spend roughly a third sleeping (ah, for the lucky ones), a third on personal matters (grooming, cleaning, reading cool business books, being with family, exercising and entertainment), and then the remaining third is spent in work. For business owners and entrepreneurs, those numbers are probably weighted much heavier to work. So, if we remove sleep for the moment, that leaves two thirds of your life interacting with people, with a third of that interaction being spent in a working environment.

All throughout the Bible we see how God strategically dealt with people in leadership roles and if they weren't there, He orchestrated their ascent. Joseph became second only to Pharaoh in Egypt. Daniel was under multiple kings during the exile period. Esther was married to one of the kings that Daniel interacted with, Xerxes. And there's more. Note, Jesus as He passes through Jericho on His way back to Jerusalem for His ultimate destiny, doesn't go to the home of just any tax collector, but rather Zacchaeus, the "director" of the tax collectors "who was rich." God knows how to get things done - get to the leaders. In this book I've tried to reach out to those who are business leaders to show that God clearly has a plan for your work lives.

I've asked you to see that God had a lot in mind for those forty plus hours a week that you spend working. He had a vision of Kingdom Business woven into the creation story. He never meant for work to be biding time or just a means to an end. He meant for us to prosper and to bless others with that prosperity. However, there are some key principles that really distinguish a regular business from a true Kingdom Business. He made sure we had the data if you will, to make our businesses and our work align with His plan and fit within His Kingdom. But this all requires vision, understanding of our Kingdom Calling.

With this knowledge, we can also make our work matter even more when we look for projects, partners, engagement of employees and an organizational structure that doesn't have us deviating from what we were called to do. Countless people can be touched for God as we work within this paradigm.

As part of being Kingdom Called, God never intended for it to exclude our families. Some folks can get out of balance in this area. However, as we delve deeper in scripture and industry advice, we learn that family should be alongside us in this wonderful adventure, rather than sit on the side to be squeezed into the non-sleeping remaining third of our time. Family is meant to learn from us, teach us, walk with us, and keep what has been built from evaporating in a generation or two. Generations can build upon each other to improve, grow, bless and be blessed.

Lastly, part of our Kingdom Calling is being rooted in our local church so that we can grow, serve and tithe. This is fundamental and cannot be overlooked or left out. And just as important, part of our Kingdom Calling is positioning our business within God's Kingdom, with its other members, so together more can be accomplished for God.

When all this is in place, we are positioned to truly harness the power of business to change the world. God would never have something we spend at least a third of our lives doing, not flow as part of His purpose for our lives. Rather, it was a part of His main design from the very beginning.

I'm curious how many of you would feel differently about your work if I said, "Guess what, today God is going to be the boss at your work and you get to be His partner for the day. After extensive interviews and a long arduous selection process, He chose *you* to have a unique leadership role in changing the world to become more like His Kingdom.

If you really believed this, I bet you would leap up before your alarm ever went off, and you'd spring eagerly into action for this one amazing, golden day of you and God making it a beautiful world. Then, after completely freaking out about what would be the right tie or outfit to wear to work with the Creator of the Universe, I bet you'd have selfies posted on every social media site possible of you and The Big Guy working it out. You'd frame one that offered your best angle of course, and have that right behind you at your desk for all to see when they came to talk with you after that incredible day. "Yep, that was my best day ever of me and God getting it done. Even if I never do another thing, that day made my life matter. I made a difference that day. Man, you should've seen the lives we saved, the hearts we helped heal, the brokenness across the world that got mended. You should've seen the business we built together. Best. Day. Ever!!!"

What if that were every day, but you just haven't realized it yet?

The Bible says in Proverbs, where people do not have vision, they will perish. This doesn't mean so much that they will die; it means they won't have a reason to get out of bed. That each day they will drag themselves to work with their shoulders shrugged and their heads hung low. There will be no *real* purpose behind what they do. They may start out with a motivation to earn money or get recognition for their successful business accomplishments, but ultimately, those rewards become very empty in life.

So, without any vision, people perish. But when people have a vision, especially when it's the vision God laid out for them, they thrive. They have a reason to get out of bed each day and they hold their heads high knowing that what they do each day matters. They are enthusiastic about each day because there is a purpose greater than themselves to which they are called. You have a Kingdom Calling, a purpose that is far greater than yourself.

It's a purpose that has not been recognized much in the body of

Christ for its Kingdom value. But there is a change that is happening. Slowly but surely, business owners are rising up and recognizing that they, like any other minister of the gospel, have been called to God's Kingdom to serve a very important role. You are there to contribute, to build and fulfill the Creation Mandate. You are there to give witness to the glory, and majesty and care of God for His people and His creation.

The pages of this book are filled with ideas that may be new and even a bit challenging for you. But if you are willing to take one step at a time, trusting in God and the leading of His Holy Spirit, He will put in your heart and in mine, an amazing vision that every day will get you out of bed with energy and a smile on your face to partner with Him in His Kingdom Calling.

It is my hope that this book will invigorate you, comfort you, inspire you and even challenge you. I hope that you will now see your work with God's eyes and that you will want to do a godly strategic analysis of your business based on the principles in Ephesians six. That you will branch out with a bold but humble spirit of learning with Kingdom projects, partnerships and that you will welcome family involvement in this unfolding story. That you will look at how to keep this blessed mandate going throughout the generations to come with all the various hues and tones of any great masterpiece.

You know, it's interesting to see how often Christ would demonstrate miraculous acts that would cause His disciples to ask Him to do it again, but He would tell them basically, "Why don't you do it?" We were made from the very beginning in His image, to create and reflect. I hope after reading this book, you'll know that you and your work matter, that your God is hoping you'll catch the vision He had from the very first minute. And that when Jesus says, "Why don't you do it?" You'll say, "Ok God, thank God it's Monday."

ABOUT THE AUTHOR

Joel Holm is a life-long learner and a strategic thinker who has always wanted to make the world a better place. Motivated by his faith, Joel has a passion to help corporations, churches and civic organizations make a genuine, long-lasting impact through creative entrepreneurial initiatives. Joel's recent book, See Life Different, has helped many people gain a fresh, hope-filled view of life. Joel has written numerous books, traveled to more than 90 countries, and studied countless models of business, charity and everything in between. From his vast and unique experiences, Joel brings a wealth of insight and learning to every forum in which he speaks and leads. For more information please contact Joel at joel@joelholm.com

.